BOOKS BY JAY R. LEACH

How Should We Then Live?
Behold the Man
The Blood Runs Through It
Drawn Away
Give Me Jesus
A Light unto My Path
Grace that Saves
The Narrow Way
Radical Restoration in the Church
Manifestation of the true Children of God
According to Pattern
Battle Cry

BATTLE CRY

Not by Might, nor by Power, but by My Spirit

JAY R. LEACH

Order this book online at www.trafford.com
or email orders@trafford.com

Most Trafford titles are also available at major online book retailers.

Scripture quotations are from the New King James Version of the Bible
copyright @ 1982 by Thomas Nelson Inc, unless otherwise noted.

Print information available on the last page.

ISBN: 978-1-4907-7634-7 (sc)
ISBN: 978-1-4907-7633-0 (e)

Library of Congress Control Number: 2016913542

Trafford rev. 08/22/2016

www.trafford.com
North America & international
toll-free: 1 888 232 4444 (USA & Canada)
fax: 812 355 4082

CONTENTS

SECTION IV. A MIGHTY CONQUEROR

THIS BOOK IS DEDICATED

TO OUR LORD AND SAVIOR,
JESUS CHRIST
AND
2 TIMOTHY 2:2 DISCIPLES
EVERYWHERE!

INTRODUCTION

As a pastor and theology educator for more than thirty-five years, I have heard the despairing cries and fears in the voices of many people in America and other parts of the world as they have sought hope and comfort. It takes little vision to see that the intensity of their cries is increasing into mere hopelessness with each passing day.

Daily we see multitudes in the news media who are emotionally shattered as government officials at every level bow to cultural pressures and wring their hands as the people demand an answer, "what is going on?" The answers from them come only in the form of more politically-correct laws without "we the people;" openly defying and rejecting the biblical laws of God. Out of utter confusion the people are striving to find their own answers. We observe daily in the streets of our cities and towns how this confusion is playing out, even in the type of person many desire for the next president of the United States. Their message: "Please! – Establishment politicians need not apply!" This attitude is reverberating in countries around the world as technology-driven globalization becomes inevitable.

It appears that people everywhere on the planet are seeking security over safety and the more promised – the more the promises are countered by acute instability in a world gone wild; as they reject the only solution, God, who created and controls all things and grants all wisdom and might (see Daniel 2:20-21). Individuals across the globe are taking notice that something big is shaping up to happen probably sooner than later! Oh! But in the midst of all the turmoil and panic, there is good news!

God's divine kingdom plan is producing the likeness of Hs Son, Jesus Christ within His true people, who are moving forward and upward like a mighty army by His Spirit.

My purpose in writing this book is to encourage and help equip New Testament believers in the churches to increase their readiness for increasing spiritual battles to be encountered in our assigned commission of:

1. *Preaching* the pure gospel to every creature [bringing them to repentance, acceptance, and a knowing relationship with Christ].
2. *Teaching* them to observe all that Christ has commanded, [bringing through *doctrinal and experiential teaching and training* all Church members to spiritual maturity and discipleship].

This is to be accomplished through the Holy Spirit and the unchanging *experiential* knowledge of Christ, biblical principles, and promises of God's Word applied to meet all spiritual, emotional, social and physical needs in our personal lives, our families, our churches and all the other institutions – in relationships, missions and ministries. Be encouraged – nothing is too hard for God! Too many churches are striving to do this *spiritual* task through *natural* means – Jesus said, *"Without Me you can do nothing."*

These time-tested foundational truths are not just for one generation, culture or special group, but they span the entire universe in their guidance and hope. We can react to all that is going on either positively through ["the knowledge of the truth"] or negatively [with the lies, untested opinions, scorn and ridiculous indignation of the world]. You will get excited as you discover the principles and stabilizing truths upon which we stand by faith in obedience to Christ's commands – like a mighty army! All accomplished through the Holy Spirit and the Word working God's kingdom plan in tandem – a Spiritual operation beyond all natural means!

We are living in the perilous times prophesied by Paul in 2 Timothy 3:1-14, and as we navigate these prophesied shifts that are bringing traumatic and drastic changes to many time-held moral boundaries – the only hope for America is Jesus Christ! Those who have been deceived by Satan may think otherwise, "But be assured, God is not mocked nor is He asleep!" A brief review of Israel's history speaks to every nation especially America and the West that God means business when He speaks! Notice His Word:

"My people are destroyed for lack of knowledge. Because you have rejected knowledge, I also will reject you from being priest for Me; because you have forgotten the law of your God, I also will forget your children" (Hosea 4:6).

I believe that expectancy of a great event gripping the world will be answered with the coming of "a great shaking" as prophesied in the Scriptures. In that shaking all nations and people that have turned their backs on God are destined to perish [unless they repent and turn back to the true and Living God]. Perish does not mean to be annihilated – or cease to exist; which is the popular thought in many quarters today is error.

What we do find in the Bible is that every single individual born into this world has an eternal spirit and soul that will live on somewhere eternally. Think about that, one million years from now all of us will be – by our own choosing either in heaven or hell. So what is holding back the inevitable? I believe:

- God's great love, grace and mercy
- The prayers of His saints in the world through the ages
- God's desire that none should perish

God's judgment on America is due – but the salvation of people is still the love of His heart. God's love gave us Jesus Christ, who died giving us the only access to God and heaven.

Several low-level shakings have happened thus far this century beginning with 9/11, that brought us to our knees – but as soon as the shock subsided a bit; we went right back to our own selfish playing. Then there is the turmoil in the Far and Middle East; and our decrease as the leading nation under God in the world. And the most recent shock, withdrawal of Great Britain from the European Union, the recent turmoil in the Middle East focused on the destruction of Christianity. Turkey [biblically Asia Minor] is the cradle of the seven Gentile churches of Revelation, Chapters 2 and A careful study of the seven churches reveals that Jesus' critique of these churches has proven to be an accurate history to this day. Here in the United States greed and narcissism is fueling a culture war, rising anarchy, independency, and all authority is suspect including that of the Holy Bible.

A call to Repentance

I will not give up on revival in this country, I believe it will come but only after we repent, humble ourselves before Almighty God, pray and seek His face [individually and corporately]. Nothing is too hard for God! (see Hosea 6:1-3).

Christ – Our only Hope

The hope that can sustain us through this storm does exist. Millions have found it through the ages as they have peered into the depths of God and His kingdom through His Spirit and the knowledge of His Word [Truth]. We can experience the same hope in Christ they found living in His unshakable kingdom. It's our individual choice! Jesus told Nicodemus that God does not exclude people, but people exclude themselves:

"He who believes in Him is not condemned; but he who does not believe is condemned already, because he has not believed in the name of the only begotten Son of God" (John 3:18).

I pray you will keep reading, because God wants to do great things in and through your life. What I have written in this book is the same thing my wife and I have shared with people on several continents and many areas of the United States. If you receive and apply the biblical principles and truths expounded upon in this book – a better and fruitful destiny awaits you. While the world spirals downward to judgment, as soldiers of the Cross we are admonished by His Spirit:

1. To truly "be saved" [salvation] (John 3:16; Romans 10:9-10).
2. To diligently "build yourselves up in the most holy faith" [sanctification] (1 John 3:16, Jude 3).
3. To faithfully "be steadfast unmovable" guiding lost souls to salvation, life and safety in Jesus Christ our Lord through living

a life of obedience and righteousness – always abiding in the wondrous love of God [in the service of our Lord] (Matthew 28:19-20).

Jay R. Leach
Fayetteville, North Carolina

Section I

LOVE LIFTED ME

(BASIC TRAINING)

Chapter One

THE POWER OF LOVE

"Now hope does not disappoint, because the love of God has been poured out in our hearts by the Holy Spirit who was given to us."

– Romans 5:5

L et's give the Most High God the highest praise, "Hallelujah!" God loves us! At best our natural righteous is as filthy rags, yet He desires an intimate relationship with each one of us. *Agape* and *Agapao* are Greek terms used in the New Testament to describe the love and attitude of God toward His Son (John 17:26); the human race in general (John 3:16; Romans 5:8); and to those who believe on the Lord Jesus Christ particularly (John 14:21).

These terms are also used to convey the Lord's will to those who are His concerning their attitude one toward another (John 13:34), then toward all human beings (1 Thessalonians 3:12; 1 Corinthians 16:14; 2 Peter 1:7). Agape expresses the essential nature of God.[1]

"He who does not love does not know God, for God is love" (1 John 4:8).

Christian love (agape/agapao)

God is the primary object of Christian love [agape] which expresses itself first of all in implicit love and obedience for Him and His commandments (see John 14:15, 21, 23; 5:10; 1 John 2:5; 5:3; 2 John 6).

Christian love whether exercised toward other believers or humanity in general is unconditional, and impossible in our own strength – but by His Spirit who was given to us. Further it is not an impulse from feelings, it does not always run with the natural inclinations, nor does it spend itself only upon those for whom something in return is expected.

- Christian love [agape] is the first fruit of the Spirit which I believe activates the other segments of the one fruit: joy, peace, patience, kindness, goodness, faithfulness, gentleness, and self-control in the believer (see Galatians 5:22-23).
- Christian love seeks the welfare of all (see Romans 15:2).
- Christian Love (agape) is self-giving and unselfish, caring about others and works no ill toward anyone (Romans 13:8-10).
- Christian love seeks opportunity to do good to all men and especially toward them that are of the household of the faith (see Galatians 6:10, 1 Corinthians 13 and Colossians 3:12-14).

God's interest in us

God's love (agapao) expresses itself in the deep and constant love relationship toward entirely unworthy humanity producing an experiential, "reverential love" in them for Him and a practical love [agapeo] for those who are partakers of the same toward Him with a desire to help others. He wants us to thoroughly understand that:

1. We must be born again, born from above; which is the only way we can be saved and enter a right relationship with Him. The unsaved person cannot understand this requirement because he or she is in the natural.
2. He will not be God among many gods. So the one true God now wants His people to know that He insists on an exclusive relationship with them. There is absolutely no middle position.

3. Idolatry is not obsolete in fact the sin of idolatry is so widely committed in America that it has subtly crept into society as a normal entity. Their names have changed, but their mission is the same as of old.
4. He wants us to love others as ourselves.
5. He wants us to submit to total dependency upon Him for everything.
6. He wants us to learn to hear His voice and obey His known will.
7. We are to have a proper relationship with Him; that is essential to hearing when He speaks to us – the salt and light of the world.
8. We are His ministers of reconciliation [every member a minister].
9. He wants us to share the gospel of Jesus Christ with the unsaved, that they may turn to Him in salvation.
10. We are to walk circumspectly in the world; enduring hardships knowing that we are in the world, but not of this world.
11. He wants us to come into the knowledge of the truth of God and Christ through His Spirit and Word.
12. He wants us to be transformed into "living sacrifices" with renewed minds and knowing what the perfect will of God is.
13. He wants us to glorify Him through our life-living before a lost world – this is His will and our purpose. Give Him praise and glory!

His love poured out

Frequently I have a conversation with a person who counts on their circumstances and experiences to know God's will. When you meet them they are looking for the [good] door of circumstances to open for them to enter. When the [bad] door opens, then they will come to us – we can help them with the truth.

One of the major problems in the church today is the fact that much of the so-called truth given out is actually second-hand stuff that we've heard but in many cases never personally checked the validity of it in the Scriptures. So is that really truth?

God's love is like a wheel hub which holds the spokes in check or together. God's Spirit and His Word work in tandem – guiding believers into the perfect will of God, through His poured out love upon us. When there is true agape love, however, it is proof of the Holy Spirit at work because:

- The flesh cannot demonstrate agape love (see Jeremiah 17:9).
- Satan cannot manifest agape love, he is full of hate (see John 8:44).
- Only the Holy Spirit can love [agape] – because we have the Holy Spirit we can love. It is up to us to prove to those around us who are longing to see Christians live out true agape love. Do you have this love?

By My Spirit

God has a tendency of giving us just enough of His will in a matter to get us started, but He operates on a need to know basis; so that we can obediently make the necessary adjustments at His leading. If we had the whole picture up front, we might get discouraged and run. But more than that only knowing a part means that we have to stay in close relationship with His Spirit to know what's next.

It has been said that knowing and following God's will is like walking by the light of a flashlight on a dark night – we can see only the distance of the illumination from the light. So we must stop if the light goes out, otherwise we go on subject to stumbling and possible injury or even death in the dark. We walk by faith not by sight.

Many people keep going on [in the flesh] no matter rather they have heard from God or not. I once read that God's straight line is a zigzag. Even when we have the known destination, we still have to be led of the Holy Spirit to get there.

We have His love, but without the Spirit of God to lead us into all truth we are still lost and powerless. So few people today even believe in the Holy Spirit! Others believe in the Spirit, but deny His participation and power. I pray that we will come into the understanding that without the Holy Spirit drawing us, we cannot be born again in the first place – so without Him what we are accomplishing is only our own [performance] in our natural power and abilities?

The Holy Spirit is the third Person of the Godhead with the Father and the Son. One God in three Persons! He is Co-equal with the Father and the Son. It is the Holy Spirit who:

- Works (I Corinthians 12:11)
- Searches (I Corinthians 2:10)
- Speaks (Acts 13:2; Revelation 2:7; II Samuel 23:2; Matthew 10:20; 1 Timothy 4:1)
- Testifies (John 15:26; Nehemiah 9:30)
- Bears witness (I John 5:6)
- Teaches (John 14:26)
- Instructs (Nehemiah 9:20)
- Reproves (John 16:8-11)
- Prays and makes intercession (Romans 8:26)
- Leads (Matthew 1:1)
- Guides the believer into all truth (John 16:13)
- Glorifies the Lord Jesus Christ (John 16:14)
- Brings about regeneration (John 3:5,6)
- Strives with men (Genesis 6:3)
- Convicts people of sin (John 16:8)
- Sends messengers from God (Isaiah 48:16)
- Calls people into ministry (Acts 13:2; 20:28)
- Directs people in the service of Christ (Acts 8:29; 10:19; 16:6, 7)
- Imparts Spiritual gifts to the members in the Body of Christ (1 Corinthians 12:7-11)

God in us

God desires to have a personal relationship with each of us. So, God Himself and the Son come and live within us through the person of the Holy Spirit. We must know the Spirit as our friend, helper, comforter, and indweller. In this way we can honor Him, He is the person of the Holy Spirit.

We find a very good example in Romans 27: God assured Paul that he would go to Rome. What a zigzag! With a word of revelation from God and knowledge of His will, Paul could encourage others even under the threat of sure death to be of good cheer! Notice love's power in a right relationship with God:

- Paul loved God
- God loved Paul
- God spoke to Paul

- Paul did what God said do

Study Romans chapter 27, if you do not have that kind of relationship with God already, pray that you may have it. Hear and adjust your life to what He says to you. Trust in the Lord with all your heart and lean not to your own understanding, but in all your ways acknowledge Him and He will direct your path (Proverbs 3:5, 6).

Faith triumphs in love

"For God so loved the world that He gave His only begotten Son, that whoever believes in Him should not perish, but have everlasting life" (John 3:16).

The hope that we have being the children of God concerning our future glory with Him will not disappoint by being unfulfilled. Neither will we be put to shame or humiliated because of our hope. We are confident of that hope because, God loves us so much He sent His Son to die for us:

- "God has poured out His love in our hearts, by the Holy Spirit who was given to us" (see Romans 5:5).
- "God *demonstrates* His own love toward us, in that while we were still sinners, Christ died for us" (see Romans 5:8).
- God Himself has placed the Holy Spirit in our hearts (v.5b).
- We were reconciled to God through the death of His Son (v.10a).
- Now having been reconciled, we shall be saved by His life (v.10b).

God loved us when we were helpless, hopeless, and ungodly enemies, how much more will He love us now that we are His children?

Rejoice in the Lord

When you have done what God has told you to do; He brings to past what He has purposed. Then you and all the people with you can *rejoice* that you have experienced God:

- Glory is the same Greek word that is translated "rejoice" in v. 12. As believers we can rejoice, glory, and boast not only in our future hope – but even in our present troubles.
- Trials and tribulations produce *endurance* when we exercise faith during physical hardship, suffering, and distress (see James 1:2,3).
- This type of faith produces its own rewards (Carefully study Matthew 5:10-12; 2 Timothy 2:12).

In some local churches today due to spiritual and biblical illiteracy many members do not understand that perseverance in trials and tribulations produces character. God works in these believers to develop certain qualities and virtues that will strengthen them and draw them closer to Him. The result is *fortified hope* which is so needed in the body of Christ during these perilous times. "O What a blessing!"

Justification [none but the righteousness]

But to him who does not work but believes on Him who justifies the ungodly, his faith is accounted for righteousness (Romans 4:5).

Paul makes it clear that in declaring a person righteous is apart from any kind of human works. If one's own efforts were the basis of salvation, then God would owe salvation as a debt. Salvation is always a gift of God's sovereign grace (see Ephesians 2:8, 9).

Being justified freely by His grace through redemption that is in Christ Jesus (Romans 3:24).

This verb *justified* comes from the Greek root word for "righteous" and means "to declare righteous." This means the repentant sinner is pardoned from the guilt and penalty of sin, and receives the imputation of Christ's righteousness to his or her account. Thus, he or she receives the positive righteousness needed to be accepted by God – based solely on the merits of Christ's righteousness [*and none of our own*]. God imputes a believer's sin to Christ's account in His sacrificial death (see Isaiah 53:4, 5; 1 Peter 2:24).

The Scripture says, *"For if when we were enemies we were reconciled to God through the death of His Son, much more, having been reconciled, we shall be saved by His life"* (Romans 5:10).

It is very important that we know, that now we are "declared righteous," and "reconciled" meaning our alienation from God has been changed. True believers are no longer enemies of God; we are at peace with God. God is not mad at us – Jesus' finished work [His death and resurrection] attests to that!

Accepting this 1st step in our *basic salvation training* by faith justifies the believer with God; it is this step that marks the only way to God – through the shed blood of Jesus Christ and His finished work.

*"Therefore, having been **justified by faith** we have **peace with God** through our Lord Jesus Christ, through whom also we have **access by faith** into this **grace**, in which we stand, and **rejoice in hope** of the glory of God"* (v.1). Emphasis added.

Jesus' resurrection brought us justification before God because His resurrection proves that God accepted His sacrificial death for us. When we believe in Jesus, God imputes His righteousness to us, and we are declared righteous before Him. Therefore, God demonstrates that He is both a righteous judge and the One who declares us righteous, our justifier (see Romans 3:26).

"For He made Him who knew no sin to be sin for us, that we might become the righteousness of God in Him" (2 Corinthians 5:21).

Jesus never committed a sin. Yet He died for our sins, [*they were nailed to the cross as He bore them for us*] so that we could be declared righteous. Give Him praise and glory!

The Effect of God's Word [Cleansing and Sanctification]

The great effect of God's Word is that of cleansing and sanctifying. The key Scripture passage that holds a number of important points for this is Ephesians 5:25-27:

Christ also loved the church and gave Himself for her, that He might **sanctify** *and* **cleanse** *her with the washing of water by the word, that He might present her to Himself a glorious church, not having spot or wrinkle or any such thing, but that it should be holy and without blemish.* Emphasis added.

Cleansing

First, the two processes of cleansing and sanctification are closely related; however, they *are not* identical. The differences between the two lie in the facts:

1. That which is truly sanctified must be absolutely pure and clean, but that which is pure and clean does not have to be sanctified.
2. It is possible to have cleanness without sanctification, but it is not possible to have sanctification without purity, or cleanness.

Second, turning back to Ephesians 5 we notice in v. 26 one main purpose for which Christ redeemed the church is *"that He might sanctify and cleanse it."* Therefore, the finished work of Christ on Calvary for the church as a whole and for each individual believer in particular, is not fulfilled until those who are truly redeemed by His death have gone through a subsequent process of cleansing and sanctification.

1. In v. 27 Paul makes it clear that *only* those Christians who have gone through this process will be *conditioned* for their final presentation to Christ as His Bride.
2. The condition Paul specifies is that of a glorious church, "not having spot or wrinkle or any such thing ….. holy and without blemish."

Thirdly, it is very important that everyone notice in this passage the means that Christ uses to cleanse and sanctify the church is *"the washing of water by the Word"* (v. 26).

1. It is God's Word that is the means of sanctifying and cleansing.
2. Notice, the operation of God's Word is compared to the washing of pure water.

The cleansing power of the Word

Even before Christ's atoning death on the cross had actually been completed – He had already assured His disciples of the cleansing *power* of the Word. He told them:

"You are already clean because of the Word which I have spoken to you" (John 15:3).

We see, then, the Word of God is a divine change agent of spiritual cleansing, compared to the washing of pure water. Adjacent to the Word is the other great agent of cleansing, *the Christian's walk,* referred to by the apostle John:

"But if we walk in the light, we have fellowship with one another, and the blood of Jesus Christ His Son cleanses us from all sin" (1 John 1:7).

Here John speaks of the cleansing power of Christ's blood, shed upon the cross to redeem us from sin. God's spiritual cleansing *always* includes these two divine components:

1. The blood of Jesus shed on the cross – Justification
2. The washing with water by His Word – Sanctification

It is important to note neither is complete without the other. Christ redeemed us through His blood – so that He might cleanse and sanctify us by His Word. John speaking of Christ says,

"This is He who came by water and blood – Jesus Christ; not only by water, but by water and the blood. And it is the Spirit who bears witness, because the Spirit is truth" (1 John 5:6).

Cleansing through the Word

We have covered the process of cleansing through God's Word; now we will go on to consider the process of sanctification. If salvation is something Christ accomplished for us, sanctification is something He accomplishes in us. To begin, it is feasible that we begin with the definition of the word sanctification which means "to make holy." To be holy means to be consecrated, dedicated, or set apart to God.

Both Paul and Peter spoke of "sanctification by the Holy Spirit" as a component of our Christian experience. Concerning these components, Paul says,

God from the beginning chose you for salvation through **sanctification** *by the Spirit and belief in the truth* (2 Thessalonians 2:13). Emphasis added.

Peter adds that Christians are,

".....elect according to the foreknowledge of God the Father, in sanctification of the Spirit for obedience and sprinkling of the blood of Jesus Christ" (1 Peter 1:2).

Christ also spoke of sanctification through the Word of God when He prayed to the Father for His disciples.

"Sanctify them by Your truth. Your Word is truth" (John 17:17).

It is very clear here that sanctification comes through the truth of God's Word.

The knowledge of the truth

People, who lived in the ages prior to Pentecost, had a great deal of knowledge about God and His grace, as seen in the Old Testament. However, that knowledge was not as all-embracing as the revelation that we receive in Christ Jesus. The Old Testament prophesied that God's grace would come to the Gentiles (Genesis 12:3), but equality with the Jews *in one body* was a secret never before revealed. We have drifted a long ways from this truth over the years.

In fact Paul through whom the Spirit revealed this truth shares in Ephesians 4 how this is possible. Dr. Martin Luther King Jr. expressed the fact that eleven a.m. on Sunday morning is by far the most segregated hour experienced in America. A noted deficiency of the church today is that she remains segregated. One of the greatest joys my wife and I experienced daily in overseas missions was the sharing, togetherness and agape love of all Christians no matter the denomination, race, or color. Yet when we return to the States it's mostly back to the same old same old.

In v. 2, He urges all believers to *walk worthy of the calling with which you were called* with all lowliness and gentleness, with longsuffering, bearing with one another in love, *endeavoring to keep the unity of the Spirit in the bond of peace. Italics added.*

Not only are we segregated in the land but in the church as well. Earlier we saw that it was Christ who made us [true believers] *righteous,* and He is concerned with our walk [conduct and behavior] before Him. The true believer's walk referenced here is impossible for us to attain in the flesh [natural]. Every New Testament believer-priest's life and walk should match the excellence of Christ's calling. The character attitudes demonstrated by Jesus when He was on the earth; Paul now assigns to every believer in (vv. 2-6):

- With all lowliness and gentleness.
- With longsuffering.
- Bearing with one another in love.
- Endeavoring to keep the unity of the Spirit.
- In the bond of peace.

It is God's Spirit and Word alone …… that is able to build up within us a strong, secure structure of faith – laid upon the foundation of Christ Himself.

There is one body [of Christ] and it is to function like a fine tuned machine maintaining *itself* and *growing up to* [maturity/ discipleship], every member so that he or she can do good works (see 1 Corinthians 12:7; and see Philippians 2:5-8), also teach others that they may yet teach others the Word of God (see 2 Timothy 2:2). Brackets are mine.

The outworking of agape

The Apostle John introduces the standard of Christian love which is the measuring rod for every expression of love which is truly self-sacrificing and giving. In 1 John 3:16, he admonishes,

"By this we know love, because He laid down His life for us. And we ought to lay down our lives for the brethren."

The believer's maturity in discipleship [the outworking of agape] is epitomized as the believer gives up his or her life as God calls us to that same standard of love for one another as Christ had for us. This is God's way of growing His Church. I stated earlier this does not come naturally, but these fruit can be cultivated in you only by the Holy Spirit, who empowers us through the Word to treat others this way *consistently.*

The Apostasy

In Hebrews 10:29, we see that sanctification is through the blood of Christ.

In this passage the apostate is addressed. The apostate is the person who has known *all* the blessings of salvation but has deliberately and openly rejected our Lord and Savior, Jesus Christ. He asks in reference to such a person:

O how much worse punishment, do you suppose, will be thought worthy who has trampled the Son of God underfoot, counted the blood of the covenant by which He was sanctified a common thing, and insulted the Spirit of Grace?

This passage shows that the true believer who continues in the faith is sanctified by the blood of the new covenant that he or she has accepted – by Christ's own blood.

Resurrection Power

Therefore listen to God's Word, summed up by Peter,

*Simon Peter, a bondservant and **apostle of Jesus Christ**. To those who have obtained like **precious faith** with us by the righteousness of **our God and Savior Jesus Christ, grace and peace** be multiplied to you in the **knowledge of God** and of **Jesus our Lord**. As His **divine power**, God has given to us all things that pertain to life and godliness, through the knowledge of Him who called us by glory and virtue, by which have been given to us exceedingly great and precious promises, that through these you may be* *partakers of the **divine nature** having escaped the corruption that is in the world through lust* (2 Peter 1:1-4).

The apostle Peter describes the following resources available to the individual disciple and corporately [the church] that will make growth in the grace and knowledge possible:

- His own apostleship – with this title Peter identifies himself as an authorized spokesman for the truth that Christ proclaimed.
- Like precious faith – any disciple with faith in Jesus Christ has the same access to the Father as any other disciple.
- The gift of righteousness (justification) – given to disciples is the righteousness of Christ Himself.
- Our God and Savior Jesus Christ – this title is derived from Peter's great confession in John 6:69.
- Grace and peace – a common greeting among Christians in the epistles that flows from the knowledge of God.
- Knowledge of God and Jesus – will grow as we mature in grace through faith, therefore we will experience grace His grace in our Christian walk.

Divine Power

*"And what is the exceeding greatness of His power toward those who believe, according to the working of His **mighty [divine] power** which He worked in Christ when He raised Him from the dead and seated Him at His right hand in the heavenly places"*(Ephesians 1:19-20).

Divine power – is the power of God used in "raising Christ from the dead" and the same power is available to the church. This divine power has provided us with the *spiritual ability* to live a life of godliness.

Divine Nature

"But also for this very reason, giving all diligence, add to your faith virtue, to virtue knowledge, to knowledge self-control, to self-control, perseverance,

to perseverance godliness, to godliness brotherly kindness, and to brotherly kindness, love.

Divine nature – is the nature that characterizes God and Christ that expresses holiness, virtue, righteousness, love and grace. As regenerated disciples of Christ with the divine nature, we can exhibit the same Christlike characteristics. I spoke in an earlier section concerning our letting our spiritual gifts outrun our development of the fruit of the Spirit. In spite of contemporary thought concerning "inclusivity," the Spirit of God can produce the fruit of the Spirit only in those who are "born again, from above" and now in Christ. The Holy Spirit has shed the *love* of God in our hearts (see John 3:3-6; Romans 5:5).

Fruit of the Spirit

"But the fruit of the Spirit is love, joy, peace, longsuffering, kindness, goodness, faithfulness, gentleness, self-control. Against such there is no law. And those who are Christ's have crucified the flesh with its passions and desires. If we live in the Spirit, let us also walk in the Spirit" (Galatians 5:22-23).

The Holy Spirit produces fruit consisting of nine character traits which are linked in a certain order. Love is the very first character trait listed in Galatian 5:22-I believe love activates the others. In other words without love the others cannot be manifested at a supernatural level.

We are born with a capacity for the fruit, but anything produced naturally is temporary and unstable. Christ not society becomes the pattern for Christian living. The fruit of the Spirit is Christlike character; which is commanded of mature disciples in the Scriptures:

1. **Love** – the Greek term is *"agape"* meaning the love of choice, referring not to emotional affection, or a familial bond, but to respect, devotion, and affection that leads to willing, self-sacrificial service (see John 15:13; Romans 5:8; John 3:16-17).
2. **Joy** – is happiness based on unchanging divine promises and kingdom realities. It is the sense of well-being experienced by one who knows all is well in his or her relationship with God. That is

joy, in spite of favorable or non-favorable life circumstances (see John 16:20-23).

3. **Peace** – is the inner calm that results from confidence in one's saving relationship with Christ. Like joy, peace is not related to one's circumstances of life (see John 14:27; Romans 8:28; Philippians 4:6-7, 9).

4. **Longsuffering** – refers to the ability to endure injuries inflicted by others and the willingness to accept irritating or painful people and situations (see Ephesians 4:2; Colossians 3:12; 1 Timothy 1:15-15).

5. **Kindness** – is tender concern for others, reflected in a desire to treat others gently, just as the Lord treats all true Christians (see Matthew 11:28-29; 19:13-14; 2 Timothy 2:24).

6. **Goodness** – is moral and spiritual excellence manifested in active kindness (see Romans 5:7; 6:10; 2 Timothy 2:24).

7. **Faithfulness** – is loyalty and trustworthiness (see Lamentations 3:22; Philippians 2:7-9; 1 Thessalonians 5:24; Revelation 2:10).

8. **Gentleness** – also translated "meekness" is a humble and gentle attitude that is patiently submissive in every offense, while having no desire for revenge or retribution.

9. **Self-control** – is the restraining of passions emotions and appetites rather than being controlled by them (see 1 Corinthians 9:25; 2 Peter 1:5-6).

Rejection of the knowledge of the truth

Hosea 4:6 says, *My people are destroyed by a lack of knowledge. Because you have rejected Knowledge I also will reject you.*

The failure of the religious leaders, including many of the prophets, would bring about their downfall. The priests **failed to teach God's law to the people:**

> *For the lips of a priest*
> *should keep knowledge,*
> *and people should seek*
> *the law from his mouth.*
> – Malachi 2:7

This negligence on the part of the priests resulted in their being the special object of God's judgment. He would terminate the priestly line. This lack of knowledge is not due to a lack of information, but from a rejection of information. A Christian or church that rejects the knowledge of God's Word faces the rejection by God Himself and destruction at the hands of the great adversary, the devil.

It's time to seek the Lord

The message that Hosea passed on to his people is very appropriate for the American Church today. Hosea warned them, "It's time to seek the Lord." Over the past few months our nation is slowly coming to the realization that our solutions without first seeking the Lord only make matters worse. Church history reflects very vividly over and over, "When you forget God, bad things happen."

When the wicked are in authority the righteous retire (hide); when the righteous rule *godliness* is revived (Proverbs 28:28).

America the Beautiful today is not the America the Beautiful that we were born in. The America founded on the spiritual and moral principles of God's Word along with laws of the nation fashioned after the moral laws of God is swiftly fading away.

If Satan can keep leaders away from the leading of the Holy Spirit and the truth of God's Word, he has the victory. The Scriptures say,

*"**Obedience** is better than sacrifice"* (1 Samuel 15:22).

Then Peter and the other apostles answered and said, *"We ought to **obey** God rather than men"* (Acts 5:29). Emphasis added throughout.

*By faith Abraham, when he was called to go out into a place which he should after receive for an inheritance, **obeyed;** and he went out, not knowing whither he went* (Hebrews 11:8).

*Since you have purified your souls in **obeying the truth** through the Spirit unto sincere love of the brethren, see that you love one another with a pure heart fervently* (1 Peter 1:22).

New Testament believer-priests [true Christians] as living sacrifices offer a four-fold sacrifice unto the Lord:

1. Offer his or her own living body (see Romans 12:1; Philippians 2:17; 1 John 3:16; 2 Timothy 4:6; James 1:27).
2. Offer praise to God continually (see Hebrews 13:15; Exodus 25:22).
3. Offer his or her substance (see Hebrews 13:2, 16; Romans 12:13; Galatians 6:6, 10; 3 John 5:8; Titus 3:14).
4. The New Testament believer-priest is also an intercessor (see 1 Timothy 2:1; Colossians 4:12).

A form of godliness

Many of our churches have a form of godliness, but deny the *power* of God. Today God's moral law [*not to be confused with the Law of Moses*] along with absolute truth and a biblical worldview have been rejected; for human secular law, relative truth and a secular worldview. These elements coming together under humankind's worldly knowledge and wisdom have no power to produce true godliness in any form.

Because they are natural these leaders have only natural cures for the world's ills. Therefore to rule, the wicked must rid the world of God and godliness! What Satan cannot destroy he contaminates. He has moved his sinful contaminating operations from the shadows into the mainstream culture and all of our founding institutions in America.

A tearless form of no God

Notice the rapid influence of the wicked and godless view of God and the things of God, not only in the American society – but in the church as well. Much of the church today wants an [emotional] experience that will not cost them anything – and they have to do nothing. But notice what this deception of Satan requires of the Christian individually and corporately:

- God, Christ, the Holy Spirit and true believers must be rejected for other gods.
- True Christianity must be blended to a religious Christianity accommodate other belief systems.
- Absolute truth must be eradicated in all forms and institutions, especially the church.
- The church's witness and influence must cease publicly.
- Unity in the church must be redefined to be inclusive.
- Evangelism [proclaiming the gospel] to every creature inside the church building only.
- Edifying one another to the level consummate with local politics.

In other words they can't let the Spirit of God take a hold of their hearts and change them. Please don't think I am implying in any manner that there should be no emotional response in a truly Spiritual experience – wow! In 2 Timothy 3:5 the apostle Paul said of them,

Having a form of godliness,
but denying
the power thereof:
from such turn away.

Daily some Christians leave theaters or a good movie on television in tears quite moved by some sorrowful scene. However, they can sit through a very moving worship service like a statue thoroughly unimpressed. This same Christian is not moved to compassion as they interact with people who are without God in this world. What a pity!

CHAPTER 1: FOR DISCUSSION:

1.   What would happen if Christians loved God more deeply in our local churches?

2.   What will be the results of not having a personal relationship with God and Christ?

3.   Discuss peace with God in conjunction with justification.

4.   Discuss determining God's will through circumstances and gaining the knowledge through the Word of God.

5.   Discuss the benefits of trials and tribulations for the Christian.

6.   Discuss the necessity and development of the "fruit of the Spirit."

7.   Think about this: The lack of biblical knowledge is not due to a lack of information, but from rejection of information.

8.   Explain in a few sentences what Paul meant by, "having a form of godliness, but denying the power thereof.

Chapter Two

O LORD! SAVE MY SOUL

"For if we have been united together in the likeness of His death, certainly we also shall be likewise of His resurrection, knowing this, that our old man was crucified with Him, that the body of sin might be done away with, that we should no longer be slaves of sin" (Romans 6:5, 6).

Our union with Christ in death is like being planted with Him. Like a seed, our sinful natures must die with Christ so that we might grow in Christ and bear spiritual fruit (John 12:24). The New Testament believer-priest's identification with Christ means being identified with His death, therefore it follows that we identify with His resurrection. It is logical then, that having died and having been raised with Christ, the believer should live a new kind of life. We are a new people (see 2 Corinthians 5:17).

The new man

Our old natural self or flesh can prove to be a formidable obstacle to our new born again spirit. The call of Christ and His cross is for us to hate our natural self life and seek every opportunity to get rid of it. He wants us to *sacrifice self* and be yielded wholly to the working of His Spirit. Many Christians are drastically unaware how the cross must work so that ultimately their natural [soul] power for living may be denied;

through sanctification, a renewal process of transformation of the soul which consists of:

- The mind which is renewed through the Word of God.
- The yielded will.
- The now transformed emotions by the Holy Spirit.
- The body quickened a living sacrifice.

If we are going to experience Christ's true life in the power and guidance of the Holy Spirit; then we must come to hate the old soulish [self] life or we will not be able to walk genuinely in the Holy Spirit. It is imperative that we realize that the basic condition for a spiritual walk is to fear our soulish self with its worldly wisdom and absolutely rely on the Holy Spirit. The war between the soul and the spirit is waged secretly but interminably within the children of God.

The soul seeks to retain its authority and move independently, while the new born again spirit strives to *breakout* and regain its lead position and authority over the soul and body in God's order. Christians cannot anticipate a walk and service pleasing to God if they have not crushed their soul life [in the flesh] by persistently denying it unconditionally and leaving it under foot in the dust. Many Christians allow their soul to mix with their spiritual experiences thus, often making them unstable in all their ways. It is obvious that such unhealthy spirit/ soul relationship will cause the believer to suffer in his or her spirituality.

Christ our High-Priest

This unstable condition between the spirit and soul takes on paramount significance in Hebrew 4:There the Holy Spirit instructs us how to divide the spirit and soul experientially. In Hebrews 4 the Holy Spirit sets forth the *high-priestly* ministry of the Lord Jesus Christ and explains its relationship to us. Verse 12 tells us that,

"The word of God is living and active, sharper than any two-edged sword, piercing to the division of soul and spirit, of joints and marrow, and discerning the thoughts and intentions of the heart."

And verse 13 follows by informing us that *"before Him no creature is hidden, but all are open and lay bare to the eyes of Him with whom we have to do."*

These Scriptures tell us how much the Lord Jesus fulfills His work as *High Priest* with respect to our spirit and soul. The Holy Spirit compares the believer with a sacrifice on the altar. The dividing of the spirit and the soul is pre-eminently a life, a must in the believer's walk. The division enables the Christian through the indwelling Spirit and Word to:

- Distinguish in experience and expressions the operations of the human spirit as distinct from that of the soul. Thus he or she may perceive what is of the spirit and what is of the soul.
- Then, through willing cooperation the Christian can follow a pure spiritual path unimpeded by the soul.
- These therefore tell us how much the Lord Jesus Christ fulfills His work as High Priest with respect to our spirit and soul.

The parting

In the tabernacle of Moses when people presented an offering, they bound their sacrifice to the altar. The priest then came and killed the animal with a sharp knife, *parting it into two and piercing to the division of the joints and marrow,* thus exposing to view all that formerly had been hidden from human sight. The blood was sprinkled on the horns [depicting power] of the altar the remainder poured out at the base. Afterward the offering was consumed on the altar with fire as an offering to God. The Holy Spirit uses this event to illustrate the offering of the Lord Jesus for sin once and for all. His shed blood on the cross of Calvary would effect salvation and liberate us from captivity, and sustained by the life of Christ. The Scripture says,

"Much more then, being now justified by His blood, we shall be saved from wrath through Him. For if when we were enemies, we were reconciled to God by the death of His Son, much more, being reconciled, we shall be saved by His life" (Romans 5:9, 10).

The good news is, we are redeemed by the blood of the Lamb out of the hands of the enemy (see I Corinthians 5:7). It is important to note what God accomplished through the shed blood of Jesus:

- His blood redeems us.
- His blood turns away judgment.
- His blood broke the power the enemy.
- His blood released us from bondage.
- His blood set us free to enter into God's promise.

Just as the sacrifice in the tabernacle was cut asunder by the priest's knife so that the joints and marrow were exposed and divided – even so the believer today has his or her soul and spirit split apart by the Word of God as wielded by our High Priest, the Lord Jesus Christ. The Word is sharper than any two-edged sword and is able to split cleanly apart the most intimately related spirit and soul; which is twisted together in reverse order because of Adam's sin. The Word pierces all the way into the innermost spirit in regeneration quickening the human spirit to live again [spiritually dead because of sin]. As your now born again human spirit is fed as the Spirit and the Word working in tandem, the spirit grows toward maturity through a personal communion in relationship with Christ (see Romans 10:9-10; 14:16-18).

Those who wish to be established in God must know the meaning of this penetration into the soul – the spirit and the soul war as the born again spirit grow spiritually and exerts increasing pressure on the soul which does not want to relinquish control gained by sin. Only the Holy Spirit can teach what soul life is and what spirit life is. Notice figure 1 below in regeneration the Holy Spirit through the Word of God *exerts outward spiritual pressure* from the spirit separating spirit and the soul [the mind is renewed, the will is yielded, and the emotions are transformed].

FIGURE #1

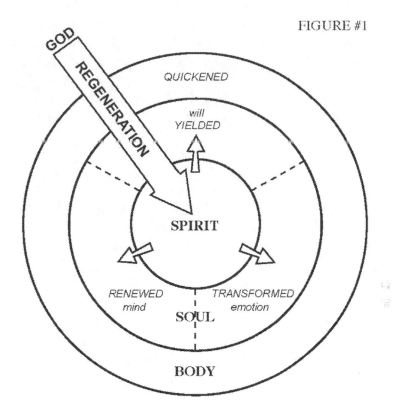

As a result of the separation the soul now *renewed through the Word* can take its rightful place of subjection to the spirit which is God's order. *Only* after the cross has done its work on the soul is the spirit truly free.

A living sacrifice

God then brings the spirit and soul back together becomes [a new heart] in union with Christ (see Hebrews 8:10-12; Jeremiah 31:31) now able to communicate with the Father, the Son and the Holy Spirit. In order to experience the parting of our soul and spirit, then we must obediently lay ourselves voluntarily upon the altar which depicts the cross of Christ, and *yielding our will* to our High Priest to do His work and lead us into a complete spiritual overhaul [sanctification]:

- Just as Jesus poured out His soul unto death (Isaiah 53:12) but committed His soul unto God (Luke 23:46), we must do the same; which will result in our too knowing, the power of the resurrection.
- Our Lord and Savior, Jesus Christ had His hands, feet and side pierced in His crucifixion. Are we willing to allow the piercing work of the cross in our soul?

Please note this separation must be known *in experience;* simply understanding in the mind will simply make us more soulish!

Thus, the soul may no longer affect the spirit nor is the spirit any longer under the soul's authority. Rather, each will find its rightful position – with neither confusion nor mixture. Having experienced the Lord Jesus' work of separation the believer must remember that this separation of their soul and spirit is based upon their having died to sin. Additionally remember, the Lord Jesus uses the gospel *teaching* of *revealed truth of His Word* to separate our soul and spirit (see Romans 12:12; 1 Corinthians 5:17).

God has made provision for us

Therefore, all Christians should maintain a daily attitude of Romans 6:1, considering themselves "dead to sin." We are not only dead to sin – but we are alive to righteousness. This must be a daily reality. It is evident that the word "therefore" in verse 12 refers back to this fact that we have died to sin; we are to no longer let sin reign in our mortal bodies. Because Christ died to sin – we died to sin. Paul means here that we have died to the "dominion of sin" or "the reign of sin."

Before we accepted Christ for salvation we were in the kingdom of Satan where we were born as a result of Adam's sin. So naturally we followed the ways of the world and its ruler, Satan (see Ephesians 2:2; Acts 26:18; and Colossians 1:13).

Paul said, referring to every person who has ever lived since Adam, except Jesus Christ, the Son of God, were born slaves in the kingdom of

Satan – but now through the shed blood and union with Christ we have been set free, rescued [*delivered*] from sin (see Romans 6:18).

Our deliverance is through our union with Christ in His death!

Our part in the next step (Sanctification)

Many Christians have a basic desire to live a sanctified life of separation unto the Lord, but have come to the conclusion that it is simply impossible. The difficulty arises for many in striving to determine their *own* part in sanctification and God's part. After many defeats of trying to live the life in their own strength most people just settle down to a life of defeat. Soon the realization comes that the old self (nature) also called (the old man or flesh) is still lurking around; trying get them to think the promises of Romans 6:6-7 are out of reach for them. This situation is causing many to give up on church today.

However, in verse 12 we can look again at God's provision in settling this problem. First we should notice in this verse that sanctification, is not allowing sin to reign in our mortal bodies is our own responsibility through the Spirit. He makes several points in his exhorting us:

- That unlike justification [by the blood] which we receive as a gift, sanctification [by the Word] is something we have to *"will"* and makes it clear we have to work at it.
- Our *will* must be influenced by the fact that we died to sin.
- We have been delivered out of the realm of sin and placed in the kingdom and realm of righteousness.
- Though God has delivered us from the reign of sin, and our old sin nature is still lurking around. Even though sin's dominion and rule are broken, the remaining sin exerts much power toward evil. According to Peter we now have a new divine nature [bury the old dead one – an old body of death lying around can still contaminate!].

As soldiers in Vietnam on several occasions we won the battle, but there were still some of the enemy soldiers around who would not give up and kept fighting. They changed their tactics to guerrilla warfare using a "hit and run" strategy and though small in number they could still inflict great damage and casualties. Long after World War II had ended some Japanese soldiers held out for years in mountains, jungles and caves, to them the war was still on.

Similarly, Satan though defeated at the cross, fights on though he knows that Christ has already won the battle for your soul denying him entrance; he can't conquer your saved soul, but he will contaminate those who are vulnerable to his tactics. The Scripture admonishes each of us to guard our heart and our life.

Instructions in righteousness

The saying goes; we are eternal students as every believer needs "instruction in righteousness." The Christian life is not a "flower bed of ease" as the old saints use to say. It is traveling upstream against strong currents of cultural and other influences. Then there are the harder-to-conquer areas that each believer has in his or her life. Many Christians find help and victory over such deer-rooted sin by becoming accountable to a pastor or another believer who will be fair and honest in progress made through structured disciplined training in righteousness. This will allow you to know the truth and the truth will set you free.

Jesus Christ, our High Priest has given us the Spirit of Truth and the Word to keep us daily, as we develop and practice our holy habits of daily devotions of prayer, Bible reading, and continuous meditation on the Word. Additionally, you should take advantage of preaching, group Bible study, discussions of God's Word, and sharing the gospel with the unsaved. In figure 2 below notice the individual's spirit is growing toward maturity as he or she follow the devotional regimen of the Word commanded of our High Priest and Lord Jesus Christ.

FIGURE #2

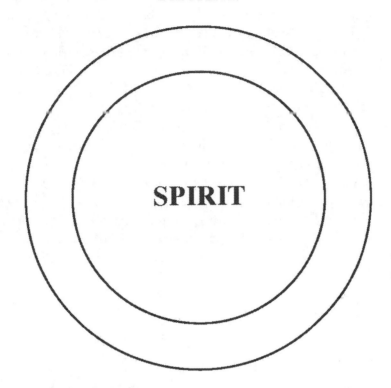

The believer is to maintain a prayerful and gracious spirit throughout the day demonstrating before the world a righteous life walking and spiritually growing by grace through faith and obedience – not by sight and self righteousness. The Word said it; I believe it and that settles it!

Satan's own

The illustration of the soldiers holding out after losing the battle holds true for Satan who has been defeated and his reign of sin has been overthrown; however he still has those who are his; who foster the death of Christianity at any cost. They specialize in secular humanism contaminating churches with erroneous theology, progressivism, secular agendas, and ruining the individual Christian's testimony through deception:

- Progressivism and their political agenda are striving to defuse and destroy true Christianity wherein biblical theology is centered on Christ, sin, repentance, guilt, salvation, the death and resurrection of Jesus, and His return for a church without spot or wrinkle. They are striving to replace it with a cold, soulish, and progressive religious Christianity.
- Progressivism's in-reach of many local churches intentionally subvert and frustrate the communication of the gospel so much and so until Christ's commission to the church is considered antiquated and obsolete today. Progressivism is not silent in expressing their agenda as they continuously judge the church as too narrow, immoral and sinful.
- This new progressivism is riding piggy-back on some of Christianity's social aspirations, especially elimination of oppression, violence, and discrimination, while at the same time striving to deconstruct all that is sacred.
- All authority is undermined in favor of individual will and expression.

Steadfast and Unmovable

Throughout church history, we find many moments when the church has weathered great cultural storms and pressures from outside elements. Over the many centuries of moral upheaval, faithful Christians and their Christian leaders have courageously stood-fast and unmovable to their theological orthodoxy.

Satanic interference was behind these activities then; as it is today. We witness the determination of radical secular humanism, atheism, and now acute progressivism which not only destroy the Christianity and the church, but also this nation and the West.

Two thousand years ago, the Spirit revealed Satan's tactic of planting his counterfeits strategically among the true believers with the intention of destroying the true Christianity through blending it with religion. Jude sounds the trumpet and calls on the saints in every generation to fight a vigorous battle to preserve the most holy faith (Jude 2-3). The first duty of every church leader is to keep the church doctrinally pure.

In spite of all the calamity the N.T. believer-priests must make their stand boldly on Romans 6:12 and not allow sin to reign in their mortal bodies. Once the spirit and soul are in union as one with the quickened body following all are now under the Lordship of Christ, with our whole heart.

In **figure 3** below we see the Christlike mature disciple who is "all heart" for God. Through love for God and others (see 1 Corinthians 13) this disciple will deny the flesh, and any opportunity to sin through the body.

FIGURE #3

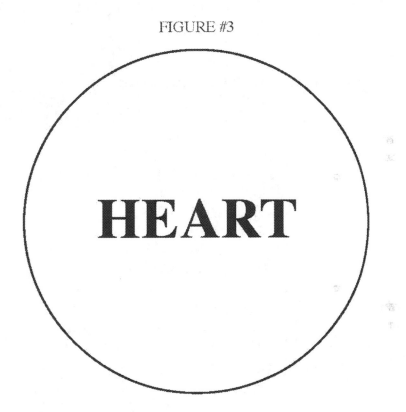

Unmovable

Herein is Christ's first line of defense of the gospel and the faith ready and unmovable Christlike believers who are spiritually mature and equipped through the Spirit and the Word working in tandem serving God in all of life.

Jude is anxious to point out that these counterfeits are **without the Spirit,** leaving no doubt of their eternal destiny. They are simply clouds without water who do not belong to God.

Notice Jude does not believe that intellectual arguments are the best defense of the gospel and the faith. While he counters with the gospel of Jesus Christ, and the essentials of "the faith," he stands on the fact that the best argument against a religious and secularized Christianity is a holy life built up in the most holy faith [salt and light]. He doe not believe in going to the law and courts, nor is he pleading for their excommunication.

The seven-fold duty of all true Christians

1. Build yourselves up in the most holy faith (see Jude 20; 1 Timothy 1:4).
2. Pray in the Spirit (see Jude 20; Ephesians 6:18; Romans 8:26).
3. Keep yourselves in the love of God (see Jude 21; 2 Timothy 1:14; Romans 8:35-39).
4. Look for the mercy of our Lord and Savior, Jesus Christ (see Jude 21; Hebrews 12:15).
5. Have compassion on some, making a difference between those who are weak spiritually and biblically, those who are proud and arrogant of heart and unwilling to obey truth (see v. 22).
6. Save the willing with fear pulling them out of the fire of eternal hell (see v. 23).
7. Here even the garment spotted by the flesh (see v. 23; James 1:27; Ephesians 5:27).

To be an effective counter force for the kingdom of God today, all believers must be mature, prayerful, teachable, and free from indwelling sin. No matter how diverse and intense the culture war may become – the best argument and deterrent to combat a paganized and secularized culture in any century is *a Spirit-filled life built up in the most holy faith.*

CHAPTER 2: FOR DISCUSSION

1. The _____ is sanctified through the revealed truth of God's Word.

2. Explain the tension between the spirit of man and the soul after conversion and cleansing.

3. Unless the soul life is _____, the Christian cannot anticipate a walk and _____ pleasing to God.

4. The piercing work of the cross is experiential; not simply an understanding in the _____.

5. God's deterrent to combat a pagan and secularized culture in any century is a _____-_____ _____ built up in the most holy faith.

6. Explain below the penetration of the soul by Christ our High Priest.

7. According to Romans 6:1, we are _____ to sin and alive to _____.

8. Briefly explain what Jude meant by "Contend for the faith once delivered to the saints.

Chapter Three

WHAT MATTERS MOST?

In various places the Scriptures compare the life of a believer to the construction of a building. For instance, the Epistle of Jude says, "Building yourselves up on the most holy faith" (v. 20). On occasion the apostle Paul uses the same picture:

You are God's building .... As a wise master builder I have laid the foundation (1 Corinthians 3:9-10).

You also are being built together for a habitation of God in the Spirit (Ephesians 2:22).

I command you .... To the word of His grace, this is able to build you up (Acts 20:32).

What matters most?

The first and most important matter to consider in constructing a permanent building is the foundation. The foundation determines the strength of the entire structure. The relationship between the foundation and the building makes them one whole. The same rule goes for the professing Christian's spiritual life. However, many begin with all of the good intentions, but sooner or later the structure may begin to sink and eventually collapse.

The reason being the relationship between the foundation and structure was not properly laid, and therefore the foundation was unable to support what was built upon it. God's only appointed foundation for the Christian's life is Jesus Christ.

Paul clearly agrees, *"For no other foundation can anyone lay than that which is laid, which is Jesus Christ"* (1 Corinthians 3:11).

Peter confirms, speaking of Christ he says, *"Therefore it is contained in the Scripture, 'Behold I lay in Zion a chief cornerstone, elect, precious"* (1 Peter 2:6).

The Solid Rock [Christ]

Now consider the words of Jesus,

When Jesus came into the region of Caesarea Philippi, He asked His disciples saying, *"Who do men say that I, the Son of Man, am?"* So they said, *"Some say John the Baptist, some Elijah, and others Jeremiah or one of the prophets."* He said to them, *"But who do you say that I am?"* And Simon Peter answered and said, *"You are the Christ, the Son of the living God."* Jesus answered and said to him, *"Blessed are you, Simon Bar-Jonah, for flesh and blood has not revealed this to you, but My Father who is in Heaven. And I also say to you that you are Peter, and on this rock I will build My church, and the gates of Hades shall not prevail against it."*

Some people suggest that these words of Jesus means that Peter is the rock upon which the Church would be built – and thus to them Peter is the foundation of Christianity rather than Christ Himself. Jesus uses a play on words to contrast Peter with a rock. In the Greek the two words sound similar, but the meaning is quite different. The name "Peter" is *Petros* and the word for "rock" is *petra.*[2] Playing upon this similarity in the sound, Jesus says, *"You are Peter [Petros] and on this rock [petra] I will build My Church."* (Matthew 16:18). Brackets are mine throughout.

Jesus Christ, therefore, is the true rock, the rock of ages, in which we find salvation. Once the foundation, Christ the Rock, has been laid in our lives, we build on that foundation by hearing and doing the Word, diligently studying the Word, and building ourselves up in the faith:

Hearing and Doing the Word

The Bible is the only authentic record we have concerning God and the things of God. You can believe every word you read in the Bible about God, about Christ, about salvation, or any other subject that has to do with your life on earth and in eternity after this life. Yes, *"faith comes by hearing, and hearing the Word of God."* (see Romans 10:17).

Failure to *feed* upon the Word of God is the reason many Christians do not hear and do, or walk by faith. Again, the Scripture says, *"But without faith it is impossible to please God: for he that comes to God must believe that He is, and that and that He is a rewarder of them that diligently seek Him"* (Hebrews 11:6).

The Scripture says, Enoch pleased God because he had faith. Without such faith it is not possible for anyone to "walk with or please God" (see Hebrews 10:38). Genuine faith is not flaky as we hear people speak from time to time. We are not talking about many Gods or many ways. Genuine faith does not just believe that a divine being exist; but that the God of the Scriptures is the only true and real God, the God of Abraham, Isaac, and Jacob. Not believing that God exist is the same as calling God a liar (see 1 John 5:10).

We must not only believe that the true God exists, but that He will reward the believer's faith in Him with forgiveness and righteousness, because He has promised to do so!

Diligent study of God's Word

Paul had led Timothy to Christ during his first missionary journey. Here he admonishes him to:

"Be diligent to present yourself approved to God, a worker who does not need to be ashamed, rightly dividing the Word of truth" (2 Timothy 2:15).

The words "diligent" and "rightly dividing" denotes tremendous persistence in accomplishing a goal. Like all preachers and teachers of the Word of God, Timothy was to give his all to impart God's Word completely, accurately and clearly to his hearers. Anything less is shameful. These instructions are very crucial to each of us who are called by God to preach and teach the Word of God; to counter false teaching (see vv. 14, 16, 17).

Built up in the most holy faith

Jude reinforces Paul's admonition: *"But you beloved, building yourselves up on your most holy faith, praying in the Holy Spirit. Keep yourselves in the love of God, looking for the mercy of our Lord Jesus Christ into eternal life"* (Jude 20, 21).

True believers have a "Solid Rock" foundation and true cornerstone in Jesus Christ. It is imperative that not only preachers and teachers but all believers be sure that Christ is their solid foundation is sure (see Ephesians 2:20). Jude gives four essentials for building themselves up:

1. Build up your lives on your most holy faith. That to be done as you are inspired in the Holy Ghost.
2. Pray in the Holy Spirit. The Holy Spirit is our inward teacher. He helps your spirits to discern the deeper things of God. He leads into all truth. He brings about that proper dependence upon God and communion with God without which the Christian life has no foundation and no substance.
3. Keep yourselves in the love of God. To do this requires human effort if God's love and power are to be effective in us.
4. Wait in quit expectancy for the mercy of the Lord; humble is the way. Be compassionate to the poor. Intercede for the lost, pulling some out of the fire.

The media is very sketchy reporting the trials Christians face daily in this country. Today it was reported that a Christian couple who refused to allow a same sex marriage ceremony to be performed on their property based on their Christian beliefs. The people undoubtedly came prepared to be turned down and recorded the conversation. Sometime later the people recorded the conversation and sued them. They were fined $13,000 dollars and warned not to not perform any weddings if they can't do both. The people were challenged to compromise their Christians values which they refused to do.

This is why Paul told the elders of the church of Ephesus:

So now, brethren, I commend you to God and to the Word of His grace, which is able to build you up (Acts 20:32). The person who builds on this foundation can say with David:

> He only is my rock and my salvation;
> He is my defense,
> I shall not be moved.
>
> – Psalm 62:6

I am reminded of Mote's old wonderful hymn of the Church:

The Solid Rock

My hope is built on nothing less Than Jesus' blood and righteousness;
I dare not trust the sweetest frame, But wholly lean on Jesus' name.
Refrain
On Christ the solid Rock I stand – All other ground is sinking sand.

CHAPTER 3: FOR DISCUSSION

1. Discuss Paul's comparison of believers and non-believers.

2. The name Peter means _____ and the word for rock is _____.

3. Discuss the Christian's foundational relationship with Christ.

4. Discuss the foundation in our lives, "that we build on Christ, the Rock."

5. Discuss David's thoughts in Psalm 62:6.

6. Review and discuss Jude's four essentials for building yourself up in the faith.

7. Keep yourself in the _____ of God.

8. Discuss the challenge facing many Christians today to compromise their Christian beliefs.

Chapter Four

LOVE IS A CHOICE

"And what agreement has the temple of God with idols? For you are the temple of the living God. As God has said:

> *"I will dwell in them*
> *And walk among them.*
> *I will be their God.*
> *And they shall be My people.*
>
>   – 2 Corinthians 6:16

Apostasy and false teaching have caused widespread compromise in much of the body of Christ to our shame today. We are not our own. God created us for His purpose and glory.

"And He has made from one blood every nation of men to dwell on the face of the earth, and has determined their pre-appointed times and the boundaries of their dwellings" (Acts 17:26).

We are to glorify God and love Him with all our heart, soul and mind; and love our neighbors as ourselves. Like so many truths in the Bible, because of self-love, spiritual and biblical ignorance many believers look at the truths of God's Word in an attitude of total defeat and unbelief.

As believers we have a foundational responsibility to love God and all of humankind. We are conduits for God's love to flow through to other human beings. In choosing God, we choose love and forgiveness in that order because God is love!

You are not forgotten

Christ died for everyone. For every sin, for every terrible thing we've done that seemed like the only choice at the time. Christ makes no exceptions. No sin is too terrible to be forgiven. There is no one whom our Savior considers unforgivable, except the *one* unpardonable sin. Jesus said,

"Every sin and blasphemy will be forgiven men, but the blasphemy against the Spirit will not be forgiven men. Anyone who speaks a word against the Son of Man, it will be forgiven him; but whoever speaks against the Holy *Spirit, it will not be forgiven him, either in this age or in the age to come"* (Matthew 12:31).

According to the study notes to the Gospel of Matthew: The sin which will not be forgiven is the stubborn refusal to heed the Holy Spirit's conviction and accept the forgiveness that Christ offers.[3] Particularly in reference to the leaders of Israel, Jesus had offered them all the proof that could be expected:

- The ministry of John the Baptist
- The testimony of the Father
- The prophesies of the Old Testament
- His own testimony
- The substantiation of the Holy Spirit

Because the leaders rejected all proofs regarding Jesus as Messiah, *nothing else* would be given.[4] It bears repeating, Jesus offers the gifts of forgiveness, salvation, and eternal life to everyone! The last verses of the Bible give one final appeal to anyone who needs Christ:

And the Spirit and the bride say, "Come!" And let him who hears say, "Come!" And let him who thirsts come. Whoever, desires, let him take of the water of life freely" (Revelation 22:17).

We need to shout it from the mountaintops above all of the false teaching, apostasy, chatter and hearsay! The forgiveness and salvation Jesus offers are gifts:

- They cannot be earned or achieved.
- You cannot be good enough to attain Jesus' forgiveness.

You are forgiven

We come to Jesus empty-handed, *"nothing in my hands I bring – only to the Cross I cling!* We are forgiven because of Christ's love, sacrifice, and compassion for us. But like any gift, the gift of forgiveness is not yours until you *choose* to repent and receive it. It's like me giving you a beautifully wrapped present and telling you all about it – you take it into your hands, but until you unwrap it and take possession of what's inside; you don't have what I wanted to give you. You can take the package home and because of the beautiful wrapping decide to put it on display for all who enter to see and admire. You can look at it periodically, yet never know what glorious gift is hidden inside.

Many of us have chosen to do the same with the *truths of God's Word.* Perhaps your Bible sits on the shelf containing God's merciful gifts of provision and blessings to you – but those blessings will never belong to you until you *choose* to receive what the Lord longs to give to you.

Put your all on the altar

In the beginning scene of creation the Word of God operated by separating light from darkness – today it works *within us* as the sword of the Spirit, piercing to the separation of the spirit and soul. God's habitation is our spirit, now separated from the fleshly desires of the soul. Perhaps this can be better illustrated through the Word itself, as the Holy Spirit compares the believer to a sacrifice on the altar.

Having been marked by the Word of the cross the soul takes its rightful place subject to the authority of the spirit. However, the soul must become a "thoroughfare" to the spirit or it can become a bond. Prior to this point the soul and spirit never agree on anything, even once the spirit has taken its rightful position it is challenged constantly by the soul.

Getting it right

We often hear people speak of the dumbing-down of our children in the public school systems. If we continue to be ignorant of the damage this discord between the spirit and soul can bring or remain unwilling to deny the flesh – we will make little if any true spiritual progress. However, we can learn much of the answer for our local churches in the ancient Jewish temple which can be likened to our whole being [spirit, soul, and body – parallels the Holy of Holies where God's glory and presence dwelt, the Holy Place where the priests worshipped daily, and the outer court where the sacrifices were offered respectively].

A curtain separated the Holy of Holies from the Holy Place. The men of that day could only know the things on the outside of the curtain in the Holy Place. Apart from faith they could only sense the presence of God. The curtain was temporary in the fact that: *at the exact hour, when the flesh of our Lord and Savior, Jesus Christ [in reality the curtain, see Hebrews 10:20] was crucified on the cross, the curtain tore from top to bottom, laying open the way to the throne of grace.* That which separated the two rooms was removed. God never planned to permanently remain in the Holy of Holies. He desired to extend His glory and presence into the Holy Place He was merely waiting for the work of the cross to be completed; which alone could rend the curtain and allow God's glory to shine forth from the Holy of Holies. It is God's intent that all of His children have such a temple experience in their spirit and soul. **If only the cross is allowed to complete its work in them.** Emphasis added.

O Lord save my soul

God tore the curtain "from top to bottom" (Mark 15:38). When the work of the cross is done God tears the curtain. There is absolutely nothing man can do to accomplish this in his own strength. Let us renew our consecration and offer ourselves fully to God. We should be willing to have our soul life committed to death in order that Christ through the Holy Spirit may finish His work in our spirit life. The Lord merges the Holy and Holiest within us just as He tore the curtain two thousand years ago so that His Holy Spirit might flow out from His glorious body. Like our spirit so shall our renewed soul [our mind, will, and emotions] be indwelt and guided by the Holy Spirit. All that we have maintained in the spirit we also now know by experience in the soul. This is Zoë, the blessed life. Therefore, the glory of God overwhelms our daily life.

"And the glory of the Lord filled the temple. And the priests could not enter the house of the Lord, because the glory of the Lord filled the Lord's house" (2 Chronicles 7:1-2).

All of our priestly activities and service in the Holy Place as we moved by faith comes to a halt now that the glorious light of God shines forth, no longer contained behind a curtain. Now that the spirit is reigning the work of the cross toward the surrender of the soul is directed toward the complete reconciliation to the spirit. When our soul is brought under subjection to the spirit by the Christ directed Word of God, it undergoes an immense *change:*

- Before the soul employed only for self seemed useless, lost and independent of God.
- Our soul after the work of the cross and the Spirit is now yielded to God. We become as **"those who have faith and keep their souls"** (Hebrews 10:39).
- Considering the magnitude of what Christ has accomplished in us through the Spirit and the Word, is much more profound than what we normally call, "saved," because it points directly to life.
- Now that we have learned not to walk by sight, we are able to save our life by faith in serving and glorifying God. **"Receive with meekness the *implanted Word,* which is able to save your souls"** (James 1:21).
- As God's Word is implanted we receive its new nature in us enabling us to bear spiritual fruit. We receive the life of the Word from the Word of life.
- Though the soul still comprise the [mind, will, and emotions] and naturally each react to various stimuli:

1. The mind engages in many thoughts and imaginations.

2. The will is antagonized by many acts of our own preference.
3. Feelings, words, environments, and manners greatly affect the emotions.

They no longer operate through the soul's power; rather they operate by the "born from above" human spirit through power of God's Spirit and Word working in tandem. This is **"the salvation of your souls"** (1 Peter 1:9). Our High Priest, Jesus Christ now brings back *together as one* in proper unity our born again spirit and renewed soul becomes our new heart.

If we are to be of use to the kingdom of God; it is imperative that this be corrective action be implemented immediately in our local churches. A little Children's Church tune goes:

Read your Bible and pray every day and you'll grow! Grow! Grow!
Don't read your Bible and pray every day
and you'll shrink! Shrink! Shrink!

I don't deserve forgiveness

When all has been said, there is always one who decides, "I don't deserve forgiveness." "My sin is too bad." "I've waited too long." "All of those wasted years, I'm not worthy of Jesus' love and compassion." I say again, **none of us deserve the forgiveness Christ offers!** Though we can never deserve eternal life – God has given us a gift called "grace:"

- Christ died on a cross [that we deserved to die on].
- As a result of His dying you and I can be forgiven of our sins [and we don't deserve it].
- God desires that we receive His gift, unwrap it and take possession of its wonderful truth.
- We love God because He first loved us. I am forgiven! Praise God!
- It is God's will for us to live forgiven lives so others can know His forgiveness through His bountiful grace.
- Love has its perfect expression among those in the Lord Jesus Christ (see 2 Corinthians 5:14; Ephesians 2:4; 3:19; 5:2).

One of the most powerful things we can do in gratitude of His love and grace at this point is bring others to Christ for their forgiveness and watch Him make their lives clean!

The law of the Spirit of life in Christ

Hopefully, you will stop beating up on yourself and get the point, stop punishing yourself for your sin. Christ has paid the price. Paul draws a contrast from Romans 7:25 with its vivid description of our prior sinfulness. Then, he depicts the freedom of living in the Spirit. In Christ we are no longer under the sentence of the law, but *empowered* by the Spirit to live for Christ. He concludes: "Therefore, there is now no condemnation for those who are in Christ Jesus, who do not walk according to the flesh, but according to the Spirit." "For the law of the Spirit of life in Christ Jesus has made me free from the law of sin and death" (Romans 8:1-2).

The law could pronounce judgment on sin – but it had *no power* to put sin to death in a person's life. God accomplished what the law could not do *by sending His own Son.* Jesus came in the likeness of sinful flesh – and took on our human nature, that was susceptible to temptation. Although He was tempted, He never sinned (vv. 3-4).

The believer gains *love,* which is the righteous standard of the law, not by means of the law but by being in Christ and walking according to the Spirit. "Love does no harm to a neighbor; therefore love is the fulfillment of the law" (v. 10).

CHAPTER 4: FOR DISCUSSION

1. Apostasy and false teaching have caused _____ _____ in much of the body of Christ.

2. God created us for His _____ and _____.

3. Scripturally discuss the unpardonable sin:

4. The _____ _____ of the Bible gave one final appeal to anyone who needs God.

5. Discuss Paul's contrast of our prior sinfulness in Romans 7:25 and the law of sin and death in Romans 8:12.

6. We are forgiven because of Christ's _____, sacrifice, and compassion for us.

7. Discuss the sinless life of Christ.

8. Discuss love as the righteous standard of the law.

Section II

FULLY COMMITTED

(ADVANCED INDIVIDUAL TRAINING)

Chapter Five

SADDLE UP SOLDIER!

For whoever wants to save his life will lose it, but whoever loses his life for Me will find it (Luke 33:17).

Therefore, wherever individual believers are obeying Christ, living out His Word in right relationship and loving Him, whether it be on the street, in the home, in the hospital, rest home or the market place, the church of Jesus Christ is vital and alive – changing the world. A mature soldier upon hearing the command "saddle up" would automatically reach for his or her weapon, [sword], the Word of God, to wield in all situations foreign and domestic. On one occasion while Paul was in jail he sent word to his friends to bring his books when they come to visit him. Today we can say book of books – the Holy Bible.

It is so sad that when asked, what is causing the spiritual decline in our culture and wider society, in survey after survey people lay the cause to a lack of Bible reading. Still being the world's best seller should indicate that it is read, but the big problem is application in our day to day lives. Those of us who have truly experienced God, Christ, and the Holy Spirit should promote the Bible; through living the truths therein, our own testimony and witness to others.

For many the Bible is just another ancient relic written thousands of years ago to cultures different than ours, how can it help with any marriage, relationships, today's parenting, financial and emotional issues of life?

I'm so glad you asked

Our God is the living Author of the Bible; He is a relational God through the Holy Spirit today to reveal the *truth* of God's Word. Advance study, training and application will prove that the Bible is relevant to our day and culture; and it can be applied to every area of our lives. We can be assured through three truths:

1. The Bible *reveals* universal truths that arm the believer with an accurate worldview.
2. It *reveals* and addresses God's expectations of how we are meant to live.
3. The Bible *meets* us at our point of need.

The remainder of this chapter will be spent acquiring a right spiritual knowledge and understanding of each of the three truths. From there the next stop in our advanced individual training will be application in the service of the Lord.

Universal truths

The demographics of our communities today have undergone tremendous change over the past fifty years or so. A major change came through the encroachment of multiculturalism mainly through business and public education. As each culture arrives it brings with it their religious beliefs along with its gods. As stated earlier America for the most part *had* a biblical worldview. People *had* a certain respect for God and the things of God which were passed down through consensus. However, the secular worldview with its no god is making great strides bent on bringing down or destroying this country.

Perceptions

Through it all we still have our beliefs about God, where we came from, where we are going and all of life in general. We process our perceptions of these things through past and present experiences of life. The end result is how we see the world and our understanding of reality.

This worldview is what we assume to be true about the basic makeup of life and the world around us.

Call it thought, persuasion or some other name, but everyone has a worldview, because everything we think or do is processed through our assumptions about how life works. These assumptions come from a variety of sources in the mix today such as:

- Religion
- Culture
- Darwinism/ evolution
- Enlightenment philosophy
- Eastern religions
- Multiculturalism
- Secularism
- Individualism
- Materialism
- Postmodernism
- Acute mechanism
- Atheism
- Naturalism

As we can see in our national and local leadership none of these philosophies provide an adequate worldview that explains the world we experience today. Certainly there is only one worldview source that clearly provides completely adequate explanations for the world as we experience it, the truth of God's Word – the Bible, the first printed book, and still the best seller of all times.

The Bible

The Bible tells God's story, an overarching story that ties together and gives meaning to everything in the entire universe and beyond. Here we find the true story about the human race:

- How we were created.
- Why we were created.
- Where we went wrong with God.
- How God came and rescued us.

- How God had a plan from the foundation of the world to restore fallen man to His original purpose.

As the Holy Spirit lays out the picture for us in the Bible, it becomes clear and we are equipped to find our story or place in God's grand epic. The history of humanity in God's grand epic of Scripture can be summarized through the following points:

- Ages past
- Creation
- The Flood
- Christ's first Coming [Christ incarnated paid the price of death to redeem humanity].
- The Church Age [The Holy Spirit came to inhabit humans to trust Christ, give them power to resist sin and live in right relationship with God].
- The Tribulation
- Christ's Second Coming
- Satan bound
- The Millennium
- Satan released
- Great White Throne Judgment
- Lake of Fire (all unsaved)
- Ages to Come

The biblical worldview assures humans of the ultimate restoration of God's original intent, including a perfect world without sin and evil – and humans who are sinless and endowed with eternal life. Now we have the big Scriptural picture of what God is doing in the world and how the nations of the world and individual lives and purpose fit into the history of the human race. Remember, history is God's story!

Certainly it gives us a completely relevant and perfectly patterned world that unveils a very specific life for believers to live. And it provides a way of knowing what truth really is; through the Spirit of truth working in tandem with the Word of God. A picture of what God meant for us to be and do based on our relationship with the Father and the Son. When we study and read the Bible as the source of our worldview we are enabled to understand:

- Who we are as humans in relationship to God.
- What makes something right or wrong?
- How God's way through the Spirit and the Word is meant to bring resolution to the physical, spiritual, relational, social, moral, ethical, economic and environmental problems encountered in life. That's it folks! Give Him praise and glory!

How we should live

More and more people see the Bible as a book of do this and don't do that laws to obey. However, God's Scriptural laws, instructions, and commands are representative of His ways. We are in His perfect will when we live according to His word and His ways. Therefore we enjoy abundant true peace and joy as we live the way God designed us to live. We were created in God's image; and as a result He has given us the capacity to will, reason, and love.

Inside out

We are relational beings, designed to love and be loved in order to enjoy God and one another. The Scripture says, "The kingdom of God is righteousness, joy and peace in the Holy Ghost." These fruit cannot be produced by the flesh and therefore can only be produced inside of us by the Holy Spirit.

Godless people have attacked the Bible for centuries, yet it still stands. Additionally, carnality in the church today has produced many marginal biblically-illiterate Christians who see the Bible negatively. Little do they know that when God says no it's for our provision and protection; just as it was for Israel. The person who builds his or her life on the Bible builds on that which cannot be shaken. God says, *"For I know the plans I have for you, plans to prosper* [provide for] *you and not to harm you* [but to protect you], plans to give you hope and a future" (Jerimiah 29:11NIV). Brackets are mine.

Stand true to the Word

It is not easy to stand true to the Word of God in days of opposition and persecution. Paul wrote, "Demas has forsaken me, having loved this present world" (2 Timothy 4:10). Like Demas many Christians are leaving the work for the world rather than face persecution. And Paul like Jeremiah and Baruch suffered persecution and trouble because of the Word (see 2 Timothy 2:8-9), but in the end, he was able to say, "I have kept the faith."

Our point of need

With all of our busy work, and other activities that allow us to drift, we are sometimes tempted to think that God has closed the door on us. We feel that He doesn't see that we are in need of strength, encouragement or affirmation that we are loved. Rest assured God, the Holy Spirit is there to meet our needs and He is pleased to allow His need-meeting presence, power and anointing to flow through us to others.

CHAPTER 5: FOR DISCUSSION

1. Discuss the Holy Spirit's role in biblical revelation.

2. The Bible is relevant. Discuss the three areas from Chapter 4 that may affect us.

3. How is multiculturalism affecting the church in America?

4. Discuss the state of the Holy Spirit's ministry today.

5. Discuss the Holy Spirit meeting us at our point of need.

6. The biblical worldview provides a way of knowing what truth really is through the working of the Spirit in tandem with the Word of God.

7. Discuss the plans God has for us according to Jerimiah 29:1.

8. Discuss Demas' and the present day Christian's love for this present world.

Chapter Six

EQUIPPED FOR THE MISSION

"Not by might nor by power, but by My Spirit, says the Lord of hosts"
(Zechariah 4:6).

"If anyone speaks, let him speak as the oracles of God. If anyone ministers, let him [or her] do it as with the ability which God supplies, that in all things God may be glorified through Jesus Christ…." (1 Peter 4:11)

The church was born and went forth with the Great Commission in the power of the Holy Spirit. The young church moved swiftly with the intention of conquering the world for Christ. Equipped for the mission the church went forth challenging the Jewish Pharisees of Israel, the mighty philosophers of Greece, and revolutionizing the Roman Empire. It was said of the church: "They have turned the world upside down and have come here also" (Acts 17:6). The gifts of the Spirit met human needs in the early church. Wherever there were people – these gifts helped resolve their needs not by human strength or resources, but by the power of God's Spirit.

THE GIFTS OF THE SPIRIIT [DIVINE ENABLEMENTS] MEET
HUMAN NEEDS IN THE CHURCH TODAY!

A Spirit-filled people

Peter was a good example of the change the Spirit can make in a person – from a timid, vacillating backslider to an aggressive witness for the Lord:

- On the day of Pentecost, he stood before the people and boldly proclaimed the truth of the Gospel.
- The Spirit changed Thomas from an overwhelming doubter to a man of strong living faith.
- The Spirit drove Jesus' disciples to the ends of the earth, witnessing for their Lord.
- The Spirit does the same today for those who are in Christ Jesus, and embrace the full doctrine of the Holy Spirit.
- In Acts 17 the Spirit gave Paul wisdom to answer the Stoic and Epicurean philosophers in Athens to whom everything was god. They had even erected an altar for the worship of "The Unknown God."

Spirit-filled Church

The strongest evil forces the devil threw against the church could not stand against the Spirit's prominence in the lives of the people of God – the same holds true for the churches today:

- Perverted men could not control the power of the Church.
- Armies could not destroy it.
- Governments could not enforce laws against it.
- Legislators could not pass edicts to stop it.

The world was facing a power it could not deal with: the Spirit of Almighty God who is the third member of the Trinity. He is co-equal with God the Father and Christ the Son. Jesus promised that the Holy Spirit would come to us – not to walk with us (Christians) but in us enabling, guiding and working through us. This work cannot be accomplished by natural means. This can become a reality in the churches today when the pastors and the teachers get Him into their thinking with emphasis – then He will get into the thinking and expectancy of the hearers.

The divine pattern

There is no record in the Book of Acts where the Spiritual gifts of the Holy Spirit went out of commission, nor did the Holy Spirit go back to heaven. According to Peter's speech on the day of Pentecost:

"The promise [the gift of the Holy Spirit] *is unto you, and to your children, and to all that are afar off, even as many as the Lord our God shall call"* (Acts 2:39). Bracket added.

At Pentecost an offering of first fruits was made (see Leviticus 23:20). The Holy Spirit came on this day as the first fruits of the believer's inheritance (see 2 Corinthians 5:5; Ephesians 1:11-14). The Holy Spirit puts the believer in communion with the Father and the Son. This indwelling of the Spirit is a beautiful promise of the New Covenant (see Jeremiah 31:33, 34), an indication not only of our repentance, and our sins forgiven, but also that the Lord has placed His law within our hearts. Those gathered into the church then, were also the first fruits of the full harvest of all believers to come after [not by might nor by power, but by My Spirit says the LORD].

The Church today

The call of God is the call to repentance, the call to salvation and deliverance; therefore, where God is truly saving people, the Word of God and the Spirit *[emphasized]* are still equipping and giving believers the Spiritual gifts severely as He wills for the building up of the body. Barna, Pew and other research groups report that only a small percentage of thousands of pastors that they have surveyed believe that the Holy Spirit's ministry and gifts are for operation in the local churches today. God never intended for His work of the church to be attempted in human strength; however, this is the great sin of the church today.

This thinking has reduced many churches to mere recreation or entertainment centers; however, the true church today is right on schedule in the divine pattern to receive the maximum of God's love and get the gifts of the Spirit functioning in their fullness and fruitfulness. The last chapter of the Book of Acts is still being written. Will it read the acts of the Holy Spirit, or the [failing] acts of human beings?

Spiritual gifts and ministry [Invite Him in!]

The apostle Paul possessed and demonstrated the gifts of the Spirit in his ministry. He also brought to the church much revelation of these gifts. It was Paul who in 1 Corinthians 12 listed the Spiritual gifts given to the churches or perhaps I should say made available to the churches, in chapter 13 he emphasized that without the love of God in our hearts all efforts are futile. In chapter 14, he gave the operation of the various gifts. Notice the flow 12 lists the various gifts given to Christians but they cannot flow into operation in Chapter 14 without going through the love of Chapter 13. Love continues to this day to be the identifier of true Christian brethren. One mark of the end time church is *cold love* and that leads to *no spirit* — as apostasy characterizes the day. In His writings to Timothy and to the Thessalonian church, Paul related the signs of the times --- events that would come to pass in the last days. In I Timothy 4:1 he said,

*"Now the Spirit expressly says that in **latter times** some will depart from the faith, giving heed to seducing spirits, and doctrines of devils."* Emphasis mine throughout.

He said this would happen not in his time, but in **latter times. Today we are living in those latter times.** Multitudes have left the faith and given heed to seducing spirits and doctrines of devils. Just recently while watching a travel log of San Antonio, as the guide was showing the rooms in one of our nation's finest hotels, they passed a room with the door partially open, I saw statues of Buddha, along with other gods that I recognized from Hinduism.

It is so appalling, just a few years ago there was a Gideon Bible in every hotel room, but today they are outlawed; however in preparing for events it seems that hotels are prepared to set up the idol god of your choice.

Our children are exposed to these same types of gods through multiculturalism in our nation's public schools, colleges and universities, yet our own Christian faith and Bibles are banned from the campuses.

Evolution is so ingrained into our culture that as people speak they use terminology and statements from that worldview as truth and no longer the theory that it really is. Additionally, in many of our local churches, Robert's Rule of Order has preempted the truth of God's Word [the Holy Bible] in doing God's business, preferring the majority vote rule over the Spirit's rule.

Walking in the Spirit

In spite of the various theologies concerning the proper walk of the Christian, the only consistent way to overcome the sinful desires of our human flesh is to live step-by-step in the power of the Holy Spirit as He works through our human spirit [inside out]. Walking each moment by faith and obedience to God's Word under the Spirit's control assures absolute victory over the desires of our sinful flesh. Paul says,

*"Walk in the Spirit, and you **shall not** fulfill the lusts of the flesh"* (Galatians 5:16) Emphasis added.

I heard a preacher illustrate walking and doing in the flesh as compared to walking and doing in the Spirit – would be like trying to dig a 50 foot long by 3 feet deep ditch with a teaspoon as compared to using an entrenching machine or back hoe to do the job. Unless our flesh [old man] is taken care of we bear within us the seeds of destruction. Until we are delivered [from the old life] the strength of our flesh is an ever-present danger to our testimony and spiritual growth to maturity.

By My Spirit

"By the cross," Paul said, "I am crucified unto the world" (see Galatians 6:14). In other words the cross where Jesus died became also the cross where we died. The shame, the rejection, and the loss Christ suffered on the cross belong not only to him, but also to all who are truly His in Christ. His cross that saves us also slays us. Anything less or any other way is pseudo-faith and really not true faith at all.

The valley of the shadow of death

It is so sad to say that research shows that the great majority of our church leaders in America walk not as those crucified with Christ, but as those who accept the world at its own value – no longer rejecting even its grosser immorality. Many are misled in the church where some preach that "old rugged cross" and others seem to have come up with "a new cross." This new cross is not the cross of the New Testament. To follow Christ there is only one way, the old rugged cross:

- The way of death unto abundant life.
- The way of repentance
- The old cross destroys the confidence in the flesh
- The old cross condemned
- The old cross brought reconciliation
- The old cross brought the Father's forgiveness and His peace

I know that this kind of language causes some to cut and run (old saying) to the new cross which:

- Accepts the worlds valuation of gross sins
- Accepts them without requiring death of the self
- Accepts and praises the "self"
- Does not bear the reproach of the old cross
- Boasts of its numerical strength
- Accepts the work of human hands above that of God
- Accepts the progressive tenets of secular humanism – man is the measure of all things

In spite of what the new cross declares the truth remains: To reach the new abundant life in Christ you must pass through the valley of the shadow of death (see John 6:68).

CHAPTER 6: DISCUSSION

1. Discuss the early churches' means of meeting needs through the gifts of the Holy Spirit.

2. Discuss the Holy Spirit's arrival on earth and His possible departure?

3. Discuss the 1st fruit offering in conjunction with Pentecost, the church, and the full harvest.

4. Compare current events in the news today with those Paul spoke of in 2 Timothy 3:

5. Contrast walking in the Spirit with walking in the flesh:

6. Discuss the call to repentance, the call to salvation and deliverance in god's plan of saving people.

7. In 1Timothy 4:1, Paul relates the signs of the times – events that would come to past in the _____ _____.

8. Paul said, "I am crucified to the world." Explain what he meant by this statement?

Chapter Seven

FIT TO FIGHT [REVIVAL]

"If My people who are called by My name will humble themselves, and pray and seek My face, and turn from their wicked ways, then I will hear from heaven, and will forgive their sin and heal their land" (2 Chronicles 7:14).

During the dedication of the temple King Solomon modeled intercessory prayer (Carefully study 6:3-42). He pleaded with God on behalf of the people and continued to pray with determination until the Lord answered. This type of prayer would be the catalyst for revival and restoration in the United States today (also see Daniel 9:3-29).

Solomon's prayer had been heard and would be answered, but there were conditions in verse 14 above. If God's people would do three things, God would answer in three ways:

If the people would:

1. Humble themselves – that is confess their sin and seek His face
2. Pray – repent
3. Turn – or come back to Him

God would:

1. Hear from heaven
2. Forgive their sin
3. Heal their land

The Lord made this promise to the whole nation of Israel; which would be an object lesson to other nations. This would give them a clear understanding about sin and its cost. We have the benefit of Scripture to observe how Israel handled God's promises as a nation, eventually going into Israel's Assyrian dispersal and Judah's Babylonian captivity.

I want to point out that Israel could pray together as a nation. But each individual member was also responsible for his or her own sin and each needed to seek God's forgiveness. God said in His Word,

> *"Behold, all souls are Mine;*
> *The soul of the father*
> *As well as the soul of the son is*
> *Mine;*
> *The soul who sins shall die."*
>
> – Ezekiel 18:4

God made it clear to Israel and to us: we may suffer as the result of someone else's sins, but we will be judged for our own. "I will judge you, O house of Israel and every one according to his [her] ways" (Ezekiel 18:30). What should be our response? "Repent and turn from all our transgressions." (v. 30)

In the promise to Israel God made provision for foreigners [individuals or nations] who embraced Him as God – He would number them with His people.

As a result of America's open rebellion and turning her back on God; we witness much travail, fear and panic as the people see the increasing daily degradation that has ethically brought down individuals, families, homes, churches, schools, all levels of government and the marketplace nationwide. Sin always has consequences.

We are all accountable to God. His message to each of us is persistent: "Therefore turn and live!" (Ezekiel 18:32)

However, men and women who have a biblically based worldview know there is yet tremendous opportunity for transforming all of these institutions by prayerfully reestablishing them on the Solid Rock, Christ, and the truths and principles of the kingdom of God.

The power of the Church

The real power of the church is the power of the preached gospel of the kingdom. Negligence in preaching the true gospel or no gospel has created a lack of respect for God's House because of a produced form of godliness that prevents the power of the gospel to be manifested. Special effort on the part of the church to preach and teach the truth of God's Word changes the hearts of people. Although sin is running rampart throughout the culture and wider society the truth would be reflected throughout!

A man in our community approached me concerning the need of a good lawyer to represent him in a legal matter. I recommended a lawyer who is a Christian gentleman of great integrity; the man was not pleased with my recommendation. As the conversation continued I gathered that he thought that a lawyer with an unsavory character would be better fitted for his case. He had a low estimate of a truthful counselor; which is about the same growing attitude of society toward the church.

Sadly many of our church leaders have little or no confidence in the supernatural power of the Holy Spirit; and as a result compromise on the many laws and activities promoting greed and immorality being proposed and passed by all levels of government. The church continues to allow the ostrich syndrome [remain in your four walls] to influence and guide them; thus, leaving the culture, community and other public affairs for the world to manage. The vacuum produced has been filled by secular humanism promoting postmodern [thought] that has displaced the biblical worldview with a secular worldview. At the same time the humanists are executing a full frontal attack on the basic foundational doctrinal truths of the church through such attitudes and clichés as, "That's just the way it is!" To be "progressive" put the philosophies scientific rationalism and the feelings of the individual above the laws of God. These attitudes are marked by such humanistic clichés as "it's my right!" "No God!" "Everyone is doing it!"

Correct doctrine

In the Great Commission, the Lord commanded the church to "make disciples," "preach" the gospel to every creature and also to "teach/ train" them all that I have commanded them to do. Through neglect and disobedience we have lost the hearts of the people; and now they are relying on the political process to pass laws favoring their sinful preferences. It is our Christian duty to vote, but also to be a part of the process and conversation and defend the faith.

Political action has its place in the believer's life – but we must be ever mindful that the political process in America is an earthly entity and definitely not our primary Source of power for influencing this nation for change. The strength of the church is the gospel and the accompanying standards of the faith to which the believer is committed. God's best deterrent against sin is still an obedient and righteously lived life before the people.

"But God be thanked, that though you were slaves of sin, yet you obeyed from the heart that form of doctrine to which you were delivered" (Romans 6:17).

In the Greek "form" means "mold" such as a craftsman would use to cast molten metal. Here form denotes "the shape" or "pattern of teaching" which resulted in their salvation experience. Doctrine has a profound affect on one's life – which tells the type of doctrine that has shaped it. Two terms are involved in salvation:

1. Conversion – refers to the human response to the gospel; which requires a commitment of the total [soul] personality, mind, emotions, and will. People respond to the gospel of the kingdom this way when they *understand* the nature of Christ's atonement, feel the guilt of conviction, love God, surrender their wills to Christ – who offers salvation.
2. Regeneration – is God's making the convert a new creation "born from above" as the human spirit is quickened or brought back to life by the Holy Spirit. The human spirit was dead as a result of Adam's sin in the Garden of Eden which broke relationship and alienated him from God. Additionally in regeneration the believer also receives of God's divine nature and a changed life.

Paul noted that the Romans had been slaves to sin, but had "obeyed from the heart that form of doctrine" – that is the gospel. Just as conversion and regeneration results in our obtaining salvation and ultimate deliverance or liberty from sin – continuous yielding of our will to God throughout life and walking in the Spirit is the key to spiritual victory (see v. 13).

The believer though no longer under the law is not free to do whatever he or she pleases. The believer is free only to do that which is consistent with the character of God. True freedom is freedom from sin – not freedom to sin!

A move of God

As stated in prior sections, the truth is, much of the church has divorced itself from the Holy Spirit; which leaves them with just a spiritless "form" of godliness. God moves on this earth through His people:

- God moves through the Holy Spirit in us as we preach, teach, and obediently live out the truths of His Word.
- God moves through us as we obey the prompting of the Holy Spirit.

The Lord told us to go preach the gospel of the kingdom; and He told us the way to do it and the results: As we go preach people will receive the truth in their hearts and be set free. That is where our power lies. God will receive glory as we influence our nation by the true preaching, teaching and living out His Word; which is the number one goal of the gospel:

For I am not ashamed of the gospel of Christ, for it is the power of God to salvation for everyone who believes, for the Jew first, and also for the Greek (Romans 1:16).

CHAPTER 7: FOR DISCUSSION

1. Discuss the specifics of King Solomon's prayer in 2 Chronicles 6:3-42.

2. Discuss the specifics of Daniel's prayer in Daniel 9:3-29.

3. Contrast the open rebellion in our nation and God's Word concerning it.

4. The power of the church is the _____ of the gospel of the kingdom.

5. Discuss the elements of the Great Commission in reference the church today:

6. Discuss the two terms *conversion* and *regeneration* which tells the type of doctrine that is in salvation.

7. The number one power of the church is the proclamation, demonstration, and application of the gospel of the kingdom.

8. Discuss the Holy Spirit's ministry executed through the believer.

Section III

LIKE A MIGHTY ARMY

(MATURITY & SERVIVE)

Chapter Eight

A SUPERNTURAL PEOPLE

"For God gave us a spirit not of fear but of <u>power</u>, and <u>love</u>, and a <u>self control</u>" (2 Timothy 1:7). ESV Emphasis is mine.

I heard a preacher say in an illustration, "If your being a Christian was deemed a crime would there be enough evidence to convict you?" In commercials we often hear, "get the real deal" which can be true or it could be false. Many times after making the transaction, we find out that we were deceived. Deception has almost become a norm in many business practices today. Not only is there deception in business, but it's one of the greatest hindrances in the church today wherein we claim to be spiritually mature disciples [supernatural people], yet emotionally many are still in [infancy].

The Proof is in the Pudding

Are we really who we say we are? Many in the local churches are deceived by pride or some access baggage from the past as they compare themselves with other brethren and arrive at the conclusion that they do not measure up. So, rather than come clean they become the great pretenders. We are still our old selves! I am reminded of a day my wife and I visited an old pastor in the hospital who was dying; as a young pastor I was very disturbed over the struggle he seemed to be putting up to stay here; as if he just didn't want to keep his appointment with the Lord.

Through the years I've seen others in that same predicament, but not of the stature of that old preacher. Some people are pillars of the church, but breakdown emotionally under load. The Apostle Paul expressed it this way,

"That you put off, concerning your former conduct, the old man which grows corrupt according to the deceitful lusts ...... and that you put on the new man which was created according to God, in true righteousness and holiness" (Ephesians 4:22, 24).

To "put off" is to peel away as in taking off old filthy clothes. This describes repentance from sin and submission to God at the point of conversion.

To put on the "new man" is not only to renew the mind in salvation, but transformation of the old to the new self which is created in the very likeness of God (see Galatians 2:20).

God called us to be soldiers not pacifists. Nowhere does the Bible give room for "cowardly" Christians. We are to be radical soldiers [a supernatural people of God] standing primarily for combat in the spiritual realm. We are living in a natural world ruled by Satan. He knows his time is short – so he is becoming bolder and bolder.

In view of the many slants and personal interpretations of Scripture today – how can you know that your view is correct? How do I recognize the Holy Spirit as authentic in me? In the Scriptural passage, Paul gives us four points of assurance: fearlessness, power, love, and self-control that indicate that we have the Holy Spirit within and know that we are not deceived. He told Timothy that God does not give us a spirit of fear.

The Greek word translated "fear" is *phobos* from which we get such words as *claustrophobia* (fear of being closed in). Paul wrote a contrast passage concerning "fear."

"For you did not receive a spirit that makes you a slave to fear, but you received the Spirit of sonship."

Too often believers fear using their gifts. They fear speaking for Christ and the gospel, ridicule, mockery, criticism, opposition and abuse. We are not to fear the ridicule and persecution that may be hurled at us because we are witnessing and ministering for Christ. The point is such feelings do not come from the Holy Spirit.

There are many believers who allow fear to control their relationship with the Lord. Fear acts as a barrier to total trust in Christ. How can we live for Christ in a world that is so evil and abusive? Let's observe Paul's four points of fearlessness, power, love, and self-control one at a time:

Fearlessness

Fearlessness is a state of mind that only the Holy Spirit can bring about. You can't work it up nor can you make yourself feel no fear. But when we are led and yielded to the Holy Spirit, He takes away all fear. When this calm comes upon you, you know you are in God's presence. One reason the devil cannot produce fearlessness is that he is full of fear himself; in fact he is the embodiment of fear. He's running scared, because he knows his time is short (Revelation 12:12).

The next time the devil brings up your past – you bring up his future!

All those who persecute and oppose us are the ones who are afraid! "Do not fear what they fear" (1 Peter 3:14). If the Holy Spirit has given you the grace of fearfulness, you have a *supernatural* inner strength which is beyond *natural* explanation.

- Total fearlessness is what Peter had on the Day of Pentecost. No fear! He was not bothered the slightest by the thousands of intimidating Jews all around him, even some with high rank.
- It was what Peter and John felt when they left the Sanhedrin as they were chosen to suffer the shame of Jesus' name (see Acts 5:41).

- It was what Elijah experienced on Mount Carmel while facing 450 of Jezebel's false prophets (1 Kings 18:27).

Again, this fearlessness can only be produced by the Holy Spirit, when it sets in – you know that it is the Spirit and not you.

Power

Supernatural power is what Jesus promised to His disciples at Pentecost:

"Behold I send the promise of My Father upon you; but tarry in the city of Jerusalem until you are endued with power from on high" (Luke 24:49).

"But you shall receive power when the Holy Spirit has come upon you; and you shall be witnesses to Me in Jerusalem, and in all Judea and Samaria, and to the end of the earth" (Acts 1:8).

It is when we begin to live and proclaim Christ – to use our gifts to bear witness for Him that the Holy Spirit enables us with enormous power in our spirit:

- Power to face the stress of difficulties and trials.
- Power to stand tall living and witnessing for Christ.
- Power to take on the job and to do it well – to the best of our ability.

Love

In chapter thirteen of Paul's first letter to the Corinthians, he points out the superiority of love for God and others over all other gifts. Further, without love no matter the gift; we are not fruitful members of the church. From Paul's point of view "I am nothing!"

Fully observed in the Scriptures I believe love activates the other gifts; and also cultivates the other eight slices of the fruit of the Spirit. Love deepens the fellowship one with another and with Christ who is the very life of the church. Love is the antithesis of self-importance or thinking of one's self more highly than one ought to think. Paul is emphasizing an underpinning truth aimed at selfish Christians everywhere [what we are means more to God than what we do]:

- Gifts count little with God in comparison to character. Many gifted individuals lack character – so we should not be deceived, there can be no real greatness of character for anyone without love.
- Much of the watered-down preaching and teaching today would lead a person to believe the highest good for us from God concerns making life easier for us individually.
- Like the Corinthians many of us are placing the highest values on the wrong things.

Paul seems to be echoing one of the most sober sayings of Jesus,

"Not everyone who says to Me, Lord, Lord,' shall enter the kingdom of heaven, but he who does the will of My Father in heaven. Many will say to Me in that day, 'Lord, Lord have we not prophesied in Your name, cast out demons in Your name, and done many wonders in Your name?' And then I will declare to them, 'I never knew you; depart from Me, you who practice lawlessness" (Mark 7: 21-23).

The Spirit of God enables

This displaced love demonstrates its real character; by their confidence and motivation in their works. Jesus was not suggesting that works are meritorious for salvation, but that true love will not fail to produce the fruit of good works. This is the precise emphasis of James 1:22-25; 2:26:

But be doers of the word, and not hearers only, deceiving yourselves. For if anyone is a hearer of the word, and not a doer, he is like a man observing his natural face in a mirror; for he observes himself, goes away, and immediately forget what kind of man he was. But he who looks into the perfect law of liberty and continues in it, and is not a forgetful hearer but a doer of the work, this one will be blessed in what he does.' For as the body without the spirit is dead, so faith without works is dead also.

In both the Old and New Testament, God's revealed truth of His Word is called "law" (see Psalm 19:7). We must remember, the presence of God's grace does not mean there is no moral law or code of conduct for New Testament believer-priests to obey. The Spirit of God enables believers to keep it; as He or she applies the principles of Scripture to their hearts they are freed from the bondage of sin and now able to obey God (see Romans 8:4).

Repeating the same principles in other Scripture passages Paul has made it clear; we have something to do in cooperating with the Spirit. Many of God's children zealously seek a consecrated walk and more abundant life but fail; why? Like the Galatians they attempt to make perfect in the flesh what was begun in the Spirit. They are substituting their own self efforts rather than completely depending upon the leading of the Holy Spirit. Trying to follow the Lord without denying the self is the root of all failures. Those who continue this path will instead of coming into spiritual maturity; begin to drift and eventually fall back into sins he or she had previously dealt with and like a cancer, these sins return with a vengeance. Dig up that old stump of "pride" or it will begin to sprout off springs. Christ clearly stated the futility of the sins of the flesh and works righteousness (see John 6:63). Notice the following observations concerning the flesh the Lord made through the Apostle Paul in the letter to the Romans:

1. "To set the mind on the flesh is death" (8:6).
2. "The mind that is set on the flesh is hostile toward God" (8:7).
3. "The flesh does not submit to God's law, indeed it cannot" (8:7).
4. "Those who are in the flesh cannot please God" (8:10).

Just as God hates unrighteousness, so He hates self-righteousness. The good acts done in the natural without the necessity of regeneration or union with Christ or dependence upon the Holy Spirit are no less carnal before God then are immorality, impurity or licentiousness. If they do not spring from complete trust in the Holy Spirit they are carnal and therefore rejected by God.

CHAPTER 8: DISCCUSSION

1. Discuss how you can recognize the Holy Spirit in the life of the believer.

2. Discuss the effects of the Holy Spirit after the Day of Pentecost.

3. The four points discussed in question 2 above can be produced by the _____ _____.

4. Discuss the Holy Spirit's action in the activation of the Spiritual gifts and the fruit of the Spirit:

5. Discuss the names of Satan as presented in this chapter.

6. Discuss the importance of Christian character to God in comparison with Spiritual gifts.

7. Jesus promised His disciples supernatural power which came to them at Pentecost. Discuss the power then and today.

8. Discuss God's view of self-righteousness.

Chapter Nine

A SUPERNATURAL WARFARE

"For we do not wrestle against flesh and blood, but against principalities, against powers, against the rulers of the darkness of this age, against spiritual hosts of wickedness in the heavenly places" (Ephesians 6:12).

P aul is urging the Ephesians to take their spiritual battle more seriously than anything that is important in this world. For example, today it seems that many Christians would sell their very soul for a ticket to an upcoming Super Bowl game or winning lottery ticket. These same individuals take Satan and his effect on their eternal future so lightly it is frightening. Like Paul we should standout, stand up and be accountable for the truth – and guard the spiritual character that Christ has given us. We are to warn people that lashing out against other humans; as if they are the real enemy is ludicrous. Additionally, their attitudes are immature as they assume that the battle which is spiritual can be fought and won using mere human resources. The Bible does not hold back on the reality of Satan:

- He's there in the beginning tempting Eve in Genesis 3:1.
- He's there in the middle urging David to be disobedient and take a census in I Chronicles 21:1.
- He's there in the end falling to the earth from heaven along with his rebellious followers in Revelation 12:9.

You can see Satan's footprint through prior chapters that without a doubt indicate his existence. For further study on Satan and his demons look them up in a Bible Concordance and I'm sure after examining the tremendous amount of referenced biblical material there will be no doubt that he is real:

- Jesus certainly knew that Satan was real. He referred to him numerous times and had a personal encounter with him in Matthew 4:1-11.
- The letters and records of the early church in the New Testament were always written with full awareness of Satan's evil presence and his deceptive activities.
- Even Jesus' opponents knew Satan was "the prince of demons" in Luke 11:15.

Traveling the world, you easily see Satan's destruction in many cultures. However, Western cultures are reluctant to acknowledge his presence because:

- Satan is very proficient at disguising and projecting himself in many ways. From Medieval times to the early 20th Century, he has convinced people that he is a lovable cartoon character dressed in red and carrying a pitchfork.
- We use him innocently as a mascot or we name our football, basketball or other teams for him [Red Devils, or Blue Devils].
- We use him as a philosophical metaphor for evil [the dark side or the secret desires of human nature].
- He deceives cultures into thinking he is a figment of their imagination.
- In earlier times Satan was satisfied lurking around in the shadows; however today he operates openly in plain sight.
- He operates his deceptions in the realms of truth as well as power (see Revelation 12:9).

Where did Satan come from?

To understand the fierce spiritual warfare we face today, it is necessary that we know where Satan came from and what his motivations are. Who is this most formidable enemy? Where did he come from? According to Job 1:6 and Colossians 1:16, he is a created being. Matthew 25:41 and Revelation 12:7 refer to him and his demons as angels.

- I'm sure that you are getting a clear picture of Satan and why we say he is a formidable foe. The two foundational Scriptures concerning Satan are Ezekiel 28 and Isaiah 14.
- In Ezekiel 28:12-13 we see that Satan was created perfect [the angel Lucifer]; his job was guardian of God's glory. Accordingly he had more power than anyone in the universe except for God (v.14)
- Lucifer was more beautiful than anything or anyone created. These attributes led to his fatal one-time downfall. The occasion of his sin – his rebellion against God was *pride* (see Isaiah 14:13; 1 Timothy 3:6).

As stated earlier, Satan was the most intelligent, and beautiful being in creation. It was his beauty and power that led to his prideful motivation. He became full of himself and desired the seat of God. He made a conscious and purposeful *choice*. The Scriptures make clear that we are all responsible for making this kind of decision (see Habakkuk 1:13; James 1:13). Isaiah 14:13-14 notes five "I will" statements that characterized his prideful rebellion:

1. I will ascend heaven the equal of God.
2. I will raise my throne above the stars of God.
3. I will sit on the mount of assembly.
4. I will ascend the heights of the clouds.
5. I will make myself like the Most High God.

We can see Satan's deceptive plan very early in Scripture. The first sin in the Garden of Eden was his motivation. He told Eve that if she ate of the tree of the knowledge of good and evil, she would be "like God" (see Genesis 3:5). He continues to this day to tempt with the same plan.

The heart of sin is to cross that line between creature and Creator and say, *"I want to be like God. I want to be the center of attraction. I want life to be about my dreams, my agenda and my fulfillment."*

The thinking of every human being has been corrupted by Adam's sin and the *selfish* satanic spirit expressed above. In this state of *thinking* humanity cannot see God – you must be "born again" (carefully study John 3).

Christ defeated Satan at Calvary, but he refuses to give up! He now focuses all of his fierce attention against all of Creation, but more specifically in contaminating Christianity and the Church of Jesus Christ [worldwide].

We don't stand a chance against Satan or his demons in our own strength. However, in Christ, through the power of the Holy Spirit who now resides in our born again spirit, his demons have to flee! We all must admit that from our earliest knowledgeable existence we have been aware of the invisible war between good and evil – through examples constantly paraded through television, cartoons, movies, and other media in general and the slippery slide of life itself until we are "in Christ." We begin by closing the gaps and resisting the Devil. Yet, many churches today after having fallen for Satan's deceptive lies are leading people to:

- Believe they can go to heaven without the "new birth" in the finished work of Christ (see Romans 10:9-10).
- Believe that salvation can be gained through self-effort, keeping religious traditions, doctrines of demons, and shady practices of men. Most people don't bother to check the Scriptures, therefore whatever is heard or taught true or false is what they believe. Spiritual and biblical illiteracy is taking its toll in our churches today
- Reject the knowledge of the truth of God's reveled Word, for a lie.
- Reject obedience and righteousness as the acceptable Christian way of life.
- Reject the Holy Spirit and His ministry.
- Reject the "inerrancy" of the Bible.

The invisible war

We tend to *think* that demonic activity has to do with some sickness or weird paranormal phenomena; and this gives us an excuse to ignore the invisible war.

We are involved in deadly supernatural warfare. When Lucifer was kicked out of heaven, he convinced a third of the angels to join in his rebellion against their Creator, God. As a result, they too were cast out of heaven.

Satan's command

Satan has formed a demonic hierarchy in the darkness where all were cast. His demonic forces are organized into a formidable rank and file army. Ephesians 6:12 informs us that this dark army consists of four divisions:

- Principalities
- Powers
- Rulers of the darkness of this world
- Spiritual wickedness in high places

The darkness behind the world's systems

Similar to armies the world over, Satan's formidable army of demons and spirits have a chain of command beginning with himself, the self-appointed head. No doubt he has divided the world into [*principalities*] regions, territories, and empires all commanded by one of his underlings [*powers*], who also have sub- power leaders under them [*rulers* of the darkness of this world] and *spiritual* wickedness].

Notice, in America and across the world everything seem to belong to a system commonly called a world – the world of sports, the world of finances, the world of politics, the world of health, and the world of medicine just to name a few. Satan is the prince of these world systems.

Although Satan has power, let us not forget; in Christ we have greater power! Therefore, the strength and effectiveness of satanic influence over these systems or [worlds] varies according to [in our case] a counter force of godliness. According to 1 John 4:4, God has given us His Holy

Spirit (on the inside), and "Greater is He that is in us than he that is in the world." I said in an earlier section, "God never intended for us to tackle Satan and his army in our own strength." In Luke 10:19 Jesus said, "Behold I give you power to tread on serpents and scorpions and over the power of the enemy: and nothing shall hurt them."

Many Churches and even some whole denominations have divorced themselves totally from the Holy Spirit and His ministry of Spiritual gifts and the fruit of the Spirit. Much of this is due to biblically illiterate Christians assimilating or co-existing with Satan and his worldly activities – actually they submit mainly by forfeiture.

I have stated before many churches are accepting people into membership who simply say they are Christians; and there is no manifestation whatsoever in their lives to substantiate their claims. This situation allows Satan's counterfeits, along with carnally-minded Christians to have free access, and eventually they easily move into key leadership positions in the church. Many of these people hinder the Lord's work simply by doing nothing, but simply holding the positions. Soon demonic manifestations of strongholds, access [psyche] baggage are introduced usually through pride, jealousy, envy, bitterness, anger, deceived minds, broken marriages, split churches and the like – all characteristics of the world. The body of Christ is Spiritual and supernatural! Worldly cures will only treat the above maladies, but they are not capable of curing them. Jesus is the only answer!

As stated in earlier sections, because of Adam's sin; these maladies can only be cured through a "rebirth." Jesus told Nichdemus, a Pharisee and ruler of the Jews, that "except a man [any person] be born again, he cannot see the kingdom of God." Nichodemus' follow-up question is asked today, "how can a person enter his or her mother's womb a second time?" Again, the necessity of the "new birth" grows out of the incapacity of the *natural man or woman* to "see" or "enter into" the kingdom of God.

Not the refined or gifted

However, gifted, moral, reformed, or refined, the natural man is absolutely *blinded to spiritual truth,* and *impotent* to enter the kingdom; for:

1. He or she can neither obey, understand, nor please – God (see John 3:3, 5, 6; 1 Corinthians 2:2:14; Romans 8:7, 8; Ephesians 2:3; Matthew 6:33).
2. The new birth is not a *reformation* of the old nature (see Romans 6:6).
3. The new birth is *a creative act* of the Holy Spirit (see John 3:5; 1;12, 13; 2 Corinthians 5:17; Ephesians 2:10; Galatians 3:24).
4. The condition of the new birth is *faith in the crucified Christ Himself* (see Galatians 2:20; Ephesians 2:10; 4:24; Colossians 1:27; 1 Peter 1:23-25; 2 Peter 1:4; 1 John 5:10-12).

"For God so loved the world,
That He gave His only begotten Son,
That whosoever believe in Him
Should not perish, but have eternal life"

-- John 3:16

The spiritual state

The Apostle John wrote this letter to first century Christians who were *acting in a way that was inconsistent with the relationship with Christ.* It's as if he was looking down through the ages at the church today, which is blending and assimilating themselves more unashamedly with the world each passing day. He *teaches* us to "Love *not* the world, or the things that are in the world. *If anyone loves the world, the love of the Father is not in him or her.* For all that is in the world, the lust of the flesh, and the lust of the eyes, and the pride of life, is not of the Father, but is of the world. And the world is passing away, and the lust of it; **but he who does the will of God abides forever** (see 1 John 2:15-17). Emphasis added.

John emphasizes the shortness of life. Life to be consumed with pride, materialism and sensual pleasure of this life, what a tragedy to invest our resources in things that will not last and end up unprepared for the next. In verse 18, John views **the rise of those who deny the truth of Christ** from within the Christian church as a **beginning of the end of all things.** Certainly this sinful profile has almost become the norm today. Is this the last hour?

Things may look dismal as we see in politics and the media, the apostle John in opposing the false teachers by asserting that all believers knew the truth. *"But you have an **anointing from the Holy One,** and you know all things. I have not written to you because you do not know the truth, but because you know it, and that **no lie is of the truth*** (v. 20). The true **Anointed, One, Jesus,** has His representatives who are anointed. As true children of God, now indwelt by the Holy Spirit, we are joined to the Anointed One and share in His anointing (see 2 Corinthians 1:21, 22). Therefore we can know all things with reference to truth and falsehood. Because the Spirit lives within us, we know all that we need to know in order to *resist the temptations* of false teachers and to live godly lives in this world. The anointing is the protection that believers have against the false teachers. The "Battle Cry" is "I'm standing!" Are you standing and ready for spiritual warfare?

Spiritual wickedness in high places

Satan's demonic forces are placed in strategic positions to rule over cities, places of employment, schools, communities and sadly churches of the world of religion. As the prince of this world's systems, Satan easily positions his demonic spirits in positions to infiltrate and influence the world and its systems physically, religiously, emotionally, politically, socially, and economically. That's why we are admonished by the Word of God to pray for those who rule over us.

We read in 1 Timothy 2:1-2, "I exhort therefore, that, first of all, supplications, prayers, intercessions, and giving thanks, be made for all men; for kings, and for all that are in authority; that we may lead a quiet and peaceable life in all godliness and honesty." "That is a promise!"

Powerful prayer produces supernatural results and will be absolutely answered promptly.

How can we make sure we are not ignorant to Satan's strategies? Without studying the Scriptures you cannot know what He is up to. Just studying carefully and prayerfully the Scriptures that are in this chapter will give you an idea of just how high the stakes really are!

We cannot afford to be apathetic. In this case ignorance of the things of God is not an asset but a liability. Before going into battle we should study and learn all we can about the enemy. We can learn and understand much about Satan's deceptive strategies and schemes by examining the meaning of his names in the Greek, as used in the Bible:

- Satan means – "adversary" (see Job 1:6-7; 1 Thessalonians 2:18).
- Devil means – "slanderer" (see 1 Peter 5:8).
- Lucifer means – "son of the morning" or "shining one" (see Isaiah 14:12).
- Beelzebub means – "lord of the flies" (Matthew 12:24).
- Belial means – "false god" (2 Corinthians 6:15).
- The evil one means – "absolute corrupt one" (1 John 5:19).
- The tempter means – "exploiter" (see 1 Thessalonians 3:5).
- The prince of this world means – "master of false systems" (see John 12:31; 1 John 5:19).
- The accuser of the brethren means – "will condemn you" (see Revelation 12:10).

Satan attacks God's Church

Satan is a master counterfeiter and comes to us in a multitude of ways. He often comes against God's work indirectly by crafting attractive alternatives to the gospel and the church; many of them contain some truth – but just enough error to taint the whole system:

- By blending some of his deceptions into the faith.
- By convincing the unsaved they don't need the gospel at all.
- By trying to fool us into living according to the world's standards even while we are convinced we are living according to the gospel.
- By producing many counterfeits to the real things of God.

The New Testament gives us the details of some of his tactics and attacks:

- He takes people captive through false philosophies and doctrines of demons (Colossians 2:8).
- He is the mastermind exposed behind false religions (1 Corinthians 10:20).

- He inspires many people in his domain to pose as ministers to lead people astray as they mix and mingle with the true servants of God (2 Corinthians 11:14-15).
- He also is the source of false doctrine through the teachings of his many deployed antichrists (see 1 John 2:18).

According to the Bible, all false ministers and all teachers of any belief other than faith in the gospel of Jesus Christ are the work inspired and influenced by the father of lies.

Satan's deceptions are aimed ultimately at making us question God, doubt his goodness and decide that he doesn't have our best interest at heart.

Not by might nor by power, but by My Spirit

No matter how formidable Satan's troops may be, Jesus has not left us ignorant of his devices nor without superior protection. As more and more churches put their trust in technology and reason rather than the Holy Spirit and the Word of God as God intended – they have no other alternative than to put their trust in worldly wisdom, weapons such as people, alliances, money, prestige, human logic, and as we see happening today as the world arms the churches in America with guns to protect them from the same fears they in fact have produced themselves. When you follow the desires of your sinful nature [which is all the world has to offer] your lives will produce these evil results.

All the above do more harm than good. Due to a lack of spirit and biblical knowledge; many people think this is the will of God. God's will is that we do what He says in His Word. When the Holy Spirit controls our lives, He will produce His kind of fruit in us: love, joy, peace, patience, kindness, faithfulness, gentleness, and self-control [for more details review page 24].

The Spirit battles the flesh, the old human nature – by shaping Christlike character in God's people.

Paul describes this process in his letter to the Galatians:

When you follow the desires of your sinful nature, your lives will produce these evil results: sexual immorality, impure thoughts, eagerness for lustful pleasure, idolatry, participation in demonic activities, hostility, quarreling, jealousy, outbursts of anger, selfish ambition, divisions, the feeling that everyone is wrong except those in your own little group, envy, drunkenness, wild parties, and other kinds of sin. Let me tell you again, as I have before, that anyone living that sort of life will not inherit the Kingdom of God.

But when the Holy Spirit controls our lives, He will produce this kind of fruit in us: love, joy, peace, patience, kindness, goodness, faithfulness, gentleness, and self-control. Here there is no conflict with the law.

Those who belong to Christ Jesus have nailed their passions and desires of their sinful nature to His cross and crucified them there. If we are living now by the Holy Spirit, let us follow the Holy Spirit's leading in every part of our lives" (Galatians 5:19-25).

Second, the Spirit equips God's people for ministry by giving us His gifts and spiritual power that can be used in part to overcome evil (see Acts 5:1-11).

Jesus inaugurated the age of the Spirit, making a fuller experience of God possible for us. This includes a continuing process of being transformed into Christlikeness by the Spirit at work within us. How do we use these truths in the battle? We will deploy them as supernatural weapons in the next chapter.

CHAPTER 9: DISCUSSION

1. Discuss Satan's origin according to the Scriptures.

2. Discuss the occasion of Satan's sin of rebellion.

3. Discuss the 5 "I wills" of Satan.

4. Discuss Satan's hierarchy of demonic forces.

5. Discuss the names of Satan as presented in this chapter.

6. Spiritual and biblical ignorance is taking its toll on the church today as the people reject the knowledge of the truth.

7. Discuss what the Word says, "Not by might nor by power, but by My Spirit."

8. Discuss God's will and the lack of spiritual and biblical knowledge.

Chapter Ten

A SUPERNATURAL WEAPONRY

"Finally my brethren, be strong in the Lord and in the power of His might."
(Ephesians 6:10)

As a child I enjoyed attending to two different denominational churches, both in the same town. My father pastored a Baptist Church and his brother my uncle McKinley was pastor of a Holiness Church. There was always a little on-going controversy concerning the external evidence or sign of the Holy Spirit's abiding power in the life of the believer. Both began with Acts 1:8,

"But you shall receive power when the Holy Spirit has come upon you; and you shall be witnesses to Me in Jerusalem, and in all Judea and Samaria, and to the end of the earth."

- For the Holiness church the evidence was the Greek word kratos [power] speaking in "tongues," belief that healing is in the Atonement of Christ (see Isaiah 53). <u>Experience through demonstrative demonstration</u>!
- For the Baptist Church the evidence was the Greek word dunimus [power] and the missionary spirit of "witness" for Jesus. We were encouraged to begin by winning our friends and kin. The fruit of the Spirit follows (see Galatians 5:22-23). <u>Doctrinal Purity and Evngelism</u>!

Both churches came out of Acts 1:8. To a point my wife and I have experienced rejection on both sides. We didn't line up with the traditions we were taught because we were part of a move of God across denominational lines, we had to move on. As a result, in 1998 the Lord led us to begin the Bread of Life Ministries International. The Bread of Life is a non-denominational teaching ministry in that we incorporate both *experience* and *doctrine* [the Holy Spirit and the Word of God] working in tandem *empowering* the believer's gifts and ministry to maturity [discipleship] for kingdom service and work. Thirty or so years ago the Evangelist would urge us to "Go to the church of your choice" next Sunday.

We need the Church

"Today the new Evangelist urges us to seek out a "Bible-believing/ Bible teaching church!" Why Bible-believing/ Bible teaching? Because much of the teaching and preaching today omits the true basic doctrines such as:

- God
- Christ
- The Holy Spirit
- Angels
- Creation
- The entrance of sin in the Garden
- The Atonement
- Salvation and justification
- The Church of Jesus Christ
- The gospel of Jesus Christ's finished work on Calvary.
- The "deeper *revealed* truth of God's Word and sanctification.
- Christ's return

The true Bible believing and teaching church is fundamentally a congregation of people who have been reconciled to God through the "new birth" in an experience of saving grace in Christ, wielded into a unity by the Holy Spirit, worshiping God and growing into fellowship and discipleship with one another in Christ. Since Pentecost the visible church has been the landmark of divine blessings.

The story is told of an infidel, a young lawyer, who went out west boasting that he was going where there were no churches, Sunday schools or Bibles. But before the end of his first year he wrote to a classmate, a young minister, begging him to come out where he was and start a church with a Sunday school and preaching. His letter further stated, "And be sure to bring plenty of Bibles. I have become thoroughly convinced that a place without Christians and Sundays, and churches and Bibles is too much like Hell for any living person to stay in!"

I have known well-meaning people who stood away from membership in church; but I have never known one who did so that did not suffer in their own spiritual life. On the day of Pentecost the three thousand people who were converted were at once baptized and added to the church. They hit the ground running, because they were immediately introduced through participation and familiarization of the four pillars for a true church.

Four essentials for a true Church

"They continued steadfastly in the apostle's doctrine and fellowship and in breaking of bread, and in prayer" (Acts 2:42).

The very familiar law of first mention in reference to the beginning of the New Testament Church should probably be reviewed in Acts 2:42 above. The first church provides a model for use today. Having its beginning at Pentecost the church grew from 120 to 3120 within hours. The church no doubt started as house churches [small groups] since they had no buildings.

Luke recorded the pillars this first New Testament Church guided by the Holy Spirit devoted themselves to. It behooves local churches everywhere to review this verse because herein lies the four foundational pillars of the church that Jesus said He would build. Therefore leaving out either one of these basic building-blocks of the foundation would leave His church incomplete. We will briefly look at each one of them:

1. The apostles doctrine
2. Fellowship
3. The breaking of bread

4. Prayer

The apostles' doctrine – teaching which includes preaching is not the same as motivational speaking and other popular forms of expression. We have the apostles teaching today in the complete Word of God – the Bible. The other pillars of the foundation depend on this one. Doctrinal purity is key in teaching God's truth upon which we are dependent for proper guidance and spiritual-maturity. It is needless to say, the church *must* continually be devoted to the teaching of the sacred Scriptures.

Fellowship – the original Greek term for fellowship is *koinonia,* refers to close relationships where people share things in common and involved continuously in one another ministries. Picture in your mind what a church would be like with the apostles' doctrine, but no fellowship. And fellowship does not mean coffee and doughnuts in the foyer on Sunday morning after service nor is it choir concerts. It is sharing life together, involved with one another in the good times and the bad times. An old saying goes, *"It's better felt than telt!"*

The breaking of bread – is set along with teaching and fellowship. We readily see that the people were baptized so now in the breaking of bread we have the two ordinances commanded by Jesus Himself; baptism and the Lord's table. Baptism represents our conversion and our dying to the old self life; and the Lord's table represents our lifelong communion with Him in worship.

Prayer – as was true of the early church, today the body must spend time together confessing their sins, interceding for others, seeking God's provision, and protection with thanksgiving for His many blessings. It bears repeating you can't have a true church if you take away any of the four foundational pillars of Acts 2:42. Over time other elements will be added to these four, but you can't have less than these four and still be a church. One important note concerning adding to the church, at some point the demands on the apostles grew along with the number of converts they needed to add others to the ministry. I feel that their process for filling this demand should be a fundamental prerequisite for all Christian leaders and workers in any capacity from the pulpit to the door. The apostles commanded the brethren to look among themselves and select seven men for the work, men and women today of:

• Honest report [character inside and outside of the church]

- Full of the Holy Ghost
- Full of wisdom

Though these seven men are not deacons as such, that office later arises to meet similar needs (see I Timothy 3:8-13). The apostle Paul provides extensive teaching on this subject in 1Timothy 5:3-16; also carefully study Titus (1-3).

The Scripture says, speaking of the church, *"For as the body is one and has many members, but all the members of that one body being many, are one body, so also is Christ.' For by one spirit we were all baptized into one body – whether Jews or Greeks, whether slaves or free – and have all been made to drink into one spirit"* (1 Corinthians 12:12-13).

All believers are baptized into the body of Christ. Christ places each new member of the body in the Holy Spirit for His care and safekeeping (see 2 Corinthians 1:22). We have all been made to drink into one spirit who dwells within us – and we are brought into a deeper relationship with Christ and the Spirit who is the power that Jesus promised would come and empower and enable them to be His witnesses in Acts 1:8.

The baptism of the Holy Spirit is not a saving experience for the unsaved; it is an empowering experience for the saved in order that he or she may be supernaturally equipped to perform his or her ministry. Many Christians are saved and have the Holy Spirit present in them, but He is there quietly waiting to be received and acknowledged. Undoubtedly these individuals have not yet made Him fully welcome, and given Him their full attention. Neither have they discovered His purpose for coming – thus robbing themselves of the gifts and power He desires to bestow upon them (carefully study John 14-16). The baptism in the Holy Spirit is receiving Him with power into our lives. Give Him praise and glory!

No perfect Church

Some people spend their entire life looking for the perfect church. But there will never be one as long as people are imperfect. Please know though, it is better to join an imperfect church than none at all. We learn from Paul's letters to the churches in his day that they were not perfect. Yet we never find Paul advising young Christians not to join the local assemblies. He did tell the churches to give up their unscriptural practices and to excommunicate certain members who were living in sin (see 2 Corinthians 6:14-18; 1 Corinthians 5:11, 12).

Church leaders today must be alert and discerning, and like Paul concerned with doctrinal and experiential purity of "the faith." Numerous pastors and teachers are compromising the purity of the faith and perverting the principles and truths of God's Word today by substituting their own schemes and ideas. Their study and meditation of God's Word mostly address "personal pleasure and nice to have material things." Rather than teaching all to adhere to Jesus' words in Matthew 6:33:

"But seek first the kingdom of God and His righteousness, and all these things shall be added to you."

To seek …… the kingdom of God and His righteousness means to desire and chose God's righteous rule on this earth (see vv. 9, 10). We can see the results of disobedience as I explained earlier in an earlier section, that "organization" has displaced the Holy Spirit and His ministry in many churches today; which allows a familiar spirit to take-over the man-made void which the Bible calls a "form of godliness" that denies the [kratos][5] power of the Holy Spirit and the Word of God. Thus, blocking the only way we can get the "truth" which sets us free to [worship in spirit and truth]. These two doctrines have greatly influenced my theology and philosophy of ministry for more than forty years as a pastor, theology instructor and author.

We need the Church

Christian churches come in many sizes, beliefs, organizational structures, missions and ministries. Research reveals more than 400,000 Protestant churches, 19,000 Catholic parishes, and 50,000 house churches open in the United States today. While there is diversity among them; they have much in common:

- Unite with others in worship
- Share a viable worldview
- A chance to give back
- A place to dispense charity
- A place to engage in community activities

- A place to be still in God's presence
- A place where a diverse group unite in one Spirit
- A place to meet God and pursue spiritual growth
- A place where we can contend for the faith
- A place where we can participate in one another ministries

We need the local church because God created us for love and communion with Him and one another – our highest calling. Church enables us to participate in group setting at least twice a week with one another. Where else can we mingle with the rich and poor, the judge and the ex-con, the learned and unlearned and creatively express our love to God in worship together? As in Christ's day we have in our churches the same two basic attitudes that He encountered:

1. Christlike attitudes and actions of love for others.
2. Pharisaical attitudes and actions of self-righteousness.

It is so sad that the pharisaical attitudes are more prevalent in number and definitely more noticeable in their flaring robes of self-importance, more secular than Christlike. Added to that statistic the Christian's reputation is not always spotless. Imagine the difference if we would concentrate more on loving others than outward appearance and rules – perhaps we should be reminded this is the calling of every Christian. One reason we fail so badly is we rely on ourselves, rather than the resources Jesus promised and delivered to us – the Holy Spirit and the Word of God working in tandem on our behalf.

The Holy Spirit and the Word

In Ephesians 6:10, Paul gives very important subsequent evidence of the Holy Spirit's empowering work in our lives! He says, "Finally my brethren, be strong in the Lord, *and in the power of His might."* So right away we see that this is a verse about the *supernatural power,* the Holy Spirit, Himself whom God has made available to the church corporately and as individual Christians in our daily walk. We are equipped for the fight with unseen, demonic powers that come to tempt us and war against our souls.

These two words *power* and *might* are very important in understanding spiritual warfare and spiritual armor. The word power in our text is taken from the Greek word *Kratos,* which is power that is *demonstrative, eruptive,* and it is *tangible.* It almost always comes with an *external* manifestation. Ephesians 1:19, 20 says, God used *kratos* power when He raised Jesus from the dead:

And what is the exceeding greatness of His power toward us who believe, according to the working of His mighty power [kratos] which He worked in Christ when He raised Him from the dead and seated Him at His right hand in the heavenly places."

God's great *Kratos,* power that raised Jesus from the dead and lifted Him by ascension back to glory to take His seat at God's right hand, is given to *every believer and is always available (see Acts 1:8; Colossians 1:29).* Knowing this to be true, Paul therefore did not pray that God's power be given to believers – but that the believers may be aware of the power [kratos] they already possess in Christ. Paul prays,

"according to the power [kratos] that works in us" (3:20).

When the conditions of vv. 16-19 are met, God's power working in and through believers is unlimited and far beyond their understanding. This is very significant because the phrase **"the power of His might"** is the same phrase used in Ephesians 6:10 – which denotes the [kratos] power that working behind the scenes to energize us for combating unseen evil powers. We have resurrection power! Emphasis added.

This power [kratos] comes to enable us to accomplish some type of supernatural task – not to just sit around twittiling our thumbs.

Notice, Paul sets things in proper order before beginning to discuss spiritual warfare with unseen forces or the *armor of God.*

1. First he dealt with the issue of power [kratos].

2. He wanted all believers to understand that without this power operating in our spiritual lives, we **cannot** engage in battle with the enemy in our own strength.

3. On the other hand, when we have this power, the devil is no match for us. Kratos is the supernatural weaponry that is at work in us.

4. As believers we are commanded by Christ to be bold witnesses, releasing the power of transforming truth. In fact the effective witness and influence of the local church remains God's place of transforming presence in the individual believer and remains His first deterrent against Satan and his evil forces.

The whole armor of God

With God's supernatural kratos power working in us — we are now ready and able to suit up and move out for battle with unseen demonic spirits that Satan dispatches to war against our souls. So Paul admonishes us,

"Put on the whole armor of God,
that you
may be able
to stand against
the wiles of the devil."

– Ephesians 6:11

"Put on" the "whole armor," from the Greek word *panoplia* which refers to the idea of permanent "fitted from head to toes;" which indicates that armor should be the believer's life-long attire. He uses the common armor worn by Roman soldiers as the analogy for the Christian's *spiritual defense* and *affirms* its necessity if one is to hold his or her position; while under attack from the wiles ["schemes"] of the devil as he:

- Opposes God's work (see Zechariah 3:1)
- Prevents God's Word (Matthew 4:6)
- Hinders God's servants [soldiers] (1 Thessalonians 2:18)
- Hinders the gospel (2 Corinthians 4:4)
- Snares the righteous (1 Timothy 3:7)
- Holds the world in his power (1 John 5:19)

After having to stand next to these impressive-looking soldiers during his imprisonments, Paul could see the Roman soldier's equipment. Despite the warfare Satan wages against us, our spiritual armor is far more superior to anything he or his demons can throw at us. God has provided our weaponry to protect, defend, and safeguard all that rightfully belongs to us. Though Satan is a formidable foe – Jesus has not left us *ignorant* of his many devices.

Therefore we have been duly *charged* to put on the whole armor of God and stand in opposition to him and any of his strategic attacks. The Bible commands:

"Therefore take up the whole armor of God that you may be able to withstand in the evil day, and having done all, to stand" (6:13). Stand therefore:

- Having your waist girded with **truth** – because Satan is a liar and the father of lies (see v. 14; John 8:44).
- Having "put on" the breastplate of **righteousness** – because righteousness or holiness is such a distinctive characteristic of God Himself, it is not hard to understand why that is the Christian's chief protection against Satan and his schemes (carefully study v.14; Isaiah 59:17; 2 Corinthians 7:1; 1 Thessalonians 5:8).
- Having your feet shod with the preparation of the **gospel of peace** – through Christ believers have peace with God and He is on their side (see v. 15; Romans 5:6-10).
- Having above all the shield of **faith** – which is the body of Christian doctrine, *trust in the Holy Spirit and God's Word* and *His promises* to "protect us from temptations of all sorts." Temptations are likened to "fiery darts" shot by the enemy and quenched by the oil-treated leather shield (see v. 16; 1 John 5:4).
- Having "put on" the helmet of **salvation** – Paul is speaking to those who are truly saved. Satan tries to destroy the believer's assurance of salvation with his weapons of doubt and discouragement. But the Christian can be strong in God's promises of eternal salvation in Scripture (study v. 17; John 6:37-39; 10:28, 29; Romans 5:10; 8:31-39; Philippians 1:6; 1 Peter 13:5).

- Having "taken in hand" the sword of the **Spirit** which is the **Word of God** God's Word is our only offensive weapon that gives victory over Satan and his strategies. The other pieces of armor listed in Ephesians 6: the belt, the breastplate, the shoes, the shield, and the helmet are intended for defense. Our only attack weapon is – the sword of the Spirit, **the Word of God,** *revealed* to us by the Holy Spirit (see v. 17; 2 Corinthians 10:3-5).

Without a through knowledge of God's Word and proper training for effective life application of it, the Christian has no weapon of attack, no weapon with which he or she can assault Satan and the powers of darkness and put them to flight. Throughout the church's existence Satan has used every means within his power to keep Christians ignorant of the true nature, authority, and power of God's Word.

The Lord Jesus Christ, our ultimate example, used God's Word as a weapon. Satan brought three main temptations against Jesus, and Jesus met and defeated each temptation of Satan with the same weapon – the sword, God's written Word (see Luke 4:1-13). In each case Jesus began His answer with the words, *"It is written"* and then quoted directly from the Scriptures.

It is very important to note: before the encounter with Satan began, Jesus was already "filled with the Holy Spirit. And after Jesus defeated Satan with the Word of God, He continued His ministry "in the power of the Spirit." The Word of God cuts through the lies of the evil one. As the psalmist declares, *"Your Word have I hid in my heart, that I might not sin against You"* (Psalm 119:11) Emphasis added throughout.

This lesson needs to be learned by every Christian today. There has never been a more urgent time when Christians need to study the Word of God especially those newly born again and those Christians who have newly been filled with the Holy Spirit. Without proper training in the Word many of these Christians often seem to believe that being filled with the Spirit somehow negates the need for diligent study and proper life application of God's Word.

Another pitfall with many Christians is though they may have some inkling of the danger, they still venture out day after day with little or no knowledge of God's Word without which they cannot know His will or His way. Only those with God's Word abiding within them will be spiritually strong and get the victory.

Otherwise, without this grace of strength victory is not possible. It is very sad that most churches treat their young people in such a childish manner that leaves then totally vulnerable and unprepared for spiritual warfare.

Without a through knowledge of the Word of God and know-how to apply it – a Christian has no weapon to attack Satan and his foes of darkness and get the victory.

The pastors of the local churches will never be exonerated from their duty to provide all of the members of their congregations with regular, systematic training in God's Word. I looked forward to Wednesday night prayer meeting and Bible study wherein I had the opportunity interact with the whole congregation. I encourage all pastors to do this no matter the size of the local church. Of course mega churches have their own ways of doing things; but most pastors can do so.

It never fails to amaze me that the world strives to knock out the church. No other institution can usurp this responsibility from the local church. Other institutions such as Bible colleges, may provide special instruction to supplement the teaching done in the local churches, but can never take their place.

The greatest need of the local churches is not more organization and programming, but simply: to be thoroughly taught, practical, regular instruction in the basic foundational doctrines, principles, and deeper truths of God's Word and how to apply them in every day Christian living. The whole of God's program of victory over Satan for His people centers on the indwelling Spirit and abiding knowledge of His Word and the ability to apply and wield it in all of life. Without that knowledge and capability, the church finds herself today in the same condition as Israel in Hosea's day – to whom the Lord admonished:

My people are destroyed
for lack of knowledge.
Because you have rejected
Knowledge,
I also will reject you

From being priest for Me;

Hosea 4:6a

Woe to the churches that make light of God's Word and reject the knowledge of God's truth:

Because you have forgotten the law
of your God,
I also will forget your children.

Hosea 4:6b

Certainly they face rejection by God Himself and danger of destruction at the hands of Satan. The priests had failed to teach God's law to the people; a special object for God's judgment. He would terminate the priestly line. Prayer and repentance is always our first line of defense:

- Hosea likens the false prophets and those who follow them to those who stumble in the dark: they are stumbling over the sin of idolatry and falling into ruin (see Hosea 4:5; 5:5).
- Isaiah warns that those who rely on their own strength will stumble and fall (Isaiah 40:30).
- Those who are led of the Lord will not stumble (Isaiah 63:13).
- The Lord will provide strength to those who stumbled in the past and now call upon them (1 Samuel 2:4).

Pray always

At the center of all spiritual warfare working in tandem with the Word of God is prayer. Jesus commanded us to pray always. Prayer is the most practical way to stay focused on the Lord; rather than become consumed with the enemy. It is reported that Jim Cymbala of the Brooklyn Tabernacle in New York was asked why people stood outside the door of his church on a Tuesday evening waiting for the doors to open so they would be among the first to find a seat for the weekly prayer meeting, he answered simply, "Your church would be filled every week,"

- If the people believed that God answered prayer;

- And things would be different after they prayed.

That's a fact! However so many have seen their prayers left unanswered and think that there are no personal benefits in prayer.

Prayer Changes People

Sadly many churches no longer see a need for prayer meetings. By the same token, many believers spend only a few minutes in prayer daily. Most prayer is sent up to ask for things. I think most of us probably started out that way coming to God to get what we wanted. We praise God one day because He answered our prayer; and then we become indifferent the next day because we didn't get what we wanted. We should know that God is sovereign and can do whatever He pleases whether we pray or not. So we will realize that the first reason for prayer is **not** to get what we want.

The Storms of Life: Stand and Fight

God allows experiences [storms] in our lives for our own spiritual benefit and growth. Many Christians are greatly hindered in their thinking that what they are going through is the results of some sin they've committed or that they are not in God's will. Not realizing that believers experience storms as do non-believers, sometimes even while they are in God's will.

Just think about it, we are drawn closer to God and our faith grows during these trials. Christians suffer just as the unsaved; we see that in hurricanes, tornados and certainly 9/11 and Charleston. From time to time the loss causes major pain and hardship right along with the rest of the people, yet many times through the pain and hardships God blesses us with a testimony in that He never leaves us. He blesses us in the midst of the storm, as we praise and trust Him in spite of circumstances! Give Him glory!

We see a good example in the disciples in Mark Jesus commands His disciples to get into the ship and go to the other side while He dismissed the people. Later as they were crossing, the wind blew against the ship causing the disciples to fear as they [toiled and rowed **under extreme pressure**] thinking that they would be lost in the storm. Later Jesus came to them walking on the water; when they saw Him they were troubled – immediately He talked with them, and said unto them,

"Be of good cheer: it is I; be not afraid." And He went up unto them into the ship; **and the wind ceased: and they were sore amazed in themselves beyond measure, and wondered** [now in His presence].

In His presence is joy unspeakable and full of glory. The scripture says, *"They considered not the* **miracle** *of the loaves:* [Feeding the 5000], *for their heart was hardened."* Yet, many still make little progress in prayer and their relationships with the Lord.

Little progress in prayer

Why so little progress in our prayers? We simply must die to self if we hope to have a prayer-answered relationship with Christ. Paul says,

"We had the sentence of death in ourselves that we should not trust in ourselves but in God who raises the dead" (2 Corinthians 1:9).

"Always carrying about in the body the dying of the Lord Jesus, that the life of Jesus also may be manifested in our body. For we who live are always delivered to death for Jesus' sake, that the life of Jesus also may be manifested in our mortal flesh" (2 Corinthians 4:10-11).

This is where many draw the line. Die they will not. On the surface the laxity of requirements for church is very attractive because of all the promises involved. When the Christ-life demands our death – the old man rises up in rebellion.

This reluctance shows up in another way, few people are very interested in the deeper life of revealed truth. These rejecters of truth include many pastors and teachers. We must give up "self." Release everything to His care.

Overcoming hindrances to Prayer

Sometimes even the most sincere Christian feels as if their prayers are not reaching the housetop. Sometimes in spite of your best attempts to practice what you've learned over time, all seems to end in frustration.

Sometimes you can't worship God, seek Him, live for Him, praise Him, thank Him, or wait on Him in peace.

Accepting these dry times as from the Lord without anger or resentment is to truly trust Him to bring good from all He allows (see Romans 8:28). Still for many this is a very frustrating experience. If this condition persists for a long period of time and is not responded to wisely, it may become life-threatening spiritually speaking; and could lead to abandoning the motivation for more of God and the things of God. To those who are discouraged, here are a few very practical suggestions and guidance for dealing with these times:

Removing the hindrances

We may be unaware of living independently from the Lord. So when we come to Him in prayer:

- He is not in all our thoughts.
- Some sin or disobedience may be unconfessed and unforsaken (see Psalm 66:10). We should agree with God immediately. Confess and gladly forsake it!
- The things of this life may be distracting you from the Lord. Perhaps with all of the hallo bolo in the news these days our focus may have been redirected away for the Lord to people and earthly matters over the heavenly. Repent and refocus.
- TV, radio or idle talk may have taken time and opportunity; so turn your attention and affection back to Him throughout the day (see 1 Corinthians 7:35).
- As a result, we may find our attention *solidly fixed* on things rather than on the Lord.
- Just continuously being in a hurry can rob us of time, or thought, or room for God, or others. Slow down and focus on Matthew 6:33.
- We may secretly resent some circumstance God permits in our life. Be honest with the Lord and confess it.
- We may be resenting Him for not giving us what we asked Him for in prayer. Be thankful.
- God offers Himself and every good thing to us!

Are we trying or trusting?

Our negative attitudes, resentment, bitterness, fear, and the unholy spirit of unbelief may have replaced our trust in the Lord and the gentleness He brings to our hearts. Just reading this partial list should show just how easy it is to dig a chasm to separates us from God.

- That chasm is bridged by releasing to Him all that separates or offends, and then return to Him.
- We may not be spending enough quality time with the Lord to allow the Holy Spirit to break our resistance and remove our attention from the earthly cares of this world.
- We must be willing to give our all to Him. We must be willing to relinquish everything to Him, let go of our desire to control things.
- We must be trusting and not trying. Just be at home in Christ. Trust Him. Allow Him to draw your affections back to Him as He wills.
- God can live fully only in those who have willingly and freely have died to self.
- Meditate on the names and characteristics of God. Remember He is worthy of all honor, worship, praise, and glory.

Appropriating God's promises

> *"For all the promises of God*
> *in Him [Christ]*
> *are yes, and in Him*
> *Amen,*
> *to the glory of God."*
>
> 1 Corinthians 1:20

"And my God shall supply all your need according to His riches in glory by Christ Jesus."

Philippians 4:19

For every need that may come into the life of any Christian, there is somewhere in the Word of God a promise that meets that need and may be claimed through faith in Christ. Therefore take these action steps:

1. Ask the Holy Spirit for guidance to the applicable promise.
2. Obediently follow instructions from the Holy Spirit by fulfilling any particular conditions accompanying the promise.
3. Live in expectancy of the fulfillment.

The key to fulfillment lies in knowing and applying the promises of God's Word. Peter states,

"His divine power has given to us all things that pertain to life and godliness, through the knowledge of Him who called us by glory and virtue, by which have been given to us exceedingly great and precious promises" (2 Peter 1:3-4).

Peter's and Paul's messages are in complete agreement. They tell us that God has already provided us with all that we will ever need for life and godliness. Our part is to appropriate it. Watch this:

The Scripture says, *"Commit your ways to the Lord, trust in Him, and He shall bring it to past"* (Psalm 37:5).

*   Our part is to "commit our ways to Him and trust Him."
*   God's part is to "bring it to past."

When the believer fulfills the two conditions above – then he or she can claim the promises. Appropriating faith is the key to mature Christian living! Amen.

The Leader and Spiritual Warfare

Leaders need to recognize the power of evil to cause conflict among the people of God. Through the Spirit and the Word of God, they should seek to prayerfully discern whether the opposition is indeed from Satan. He or she must know that the battle is on a spiritual level and that the weapons to use are spiritual and are derived from the Lord's victorious battle – His finished work. Every leader must conclude that; evil is not to be:

- Feared
- Ignored
- Shrunk from

But evil must be:

- Exposed
- Confronted
- Overcome
- Used for the glory of God

Hence, I found out that prayer is coming to God to receive what He wants to give us. This is one reason why Satan so bitterly tries to obstruct the preaching of the cross – especially in the aspects of Romans 6 and Colossians 2:15 on behalf of yourself and others.

Having disarmed principalities and powers,
He made a public spectacle of them,
trumping over them in it.

And Jesus said, *"Behold I give you the authority to trample on serpents and scorpions, and over all the powers of the enemy, and nothing shall by any means hurt you"* (Luke 10:19).

There are various ways of exercising this authority of Christ, the soldier stands on the basis of (Romans 6:11).

"Likewise you, also, reckon yourselves to be dead indeed to sin, but alive to God in Christ Jesus our Lord."

Reckon is an accounting term that means "to take into" "to calculate." In verses 3-10 the truth is revealed that believers have already died to sin because they have participated in Jesus' death. Since believers have died with Christ and have also been raised with Him, Paul now urges Christians to consider themselves **dead ... to sin.** Considering the fact that before conversion they were still enslaved to the power of sin – now they are free to resist it.

*"Reckoning himself in the place where alone he is out of reach of the enemy, may, **in the name of Christ,** command the evil spirit to come out"* (Luke 10:17). Emphasis added.

Christ won the victory over the demon forces on the cross, where their efforts to halt God's redemptive plan were ultimately defeated. Believers' sins were all put on Christ and nailed to His cross as He paid the penalty in their place for all of them, therefore satisfying the just wrath of God against crimes requiring full punishment.

CHAPTER 10: DISCUSSION

1. Discuss the deeper revelation truth of God's Word as discussed in chapter 9:

2. Discuss the power that raised Jesus from the dead and how that same power affects the believer today:

3. We cannot engage in battle with the enemy in our own _____.

4. Kratos is the _____ that is in us.

5. List the 6 pieces of armor in Ephesians 6:
    1.
    2.
    3.
    4.
    5.
    6.

Section IV

A MIGHTY CONQUEROR

Chapter Eleven

A SUPERNATURAL VICTORY "IN CHRIST"

A nd Jesus came and spoke to them, saying, *"All authority has been given to Me in heaven and on earth"* (Matthew 28:18).

We come to chapter eleven fighting from victory not fighting to victory. The Great Commission is not just an order but a pronouncement of victory by the risen Savior through *us,* His disciples. The triumphant living Lord now sends His ambassadors to proclaim the gospel with authority, not to the house of Israel but instead to carry out the Great Commission of the church throughout the whole world. The church is not to merely be missionary-minded, but to be Christ's means for the entire missionary effort.

Christ's formula for victory

The Great <u>Commission</u> or command carries within it the Lord's own formula for victoriously completing our assigned destiny as the body of Christ:

- "Go" – which conveys the force of a command to – "make disciples."
- "Teach all nations" – can be translated "disciple all nations," indicating the converting power of the gospel.

- "Baptizing them" – this is the *first step* of outward obedience to the Lord's command. The converts are to be baptized in the name of the Father, and of the Son, and of the Holy Ghost.
- "Teaching them" – to observe all things that I have commanded you. Notice the *second step,* teaching them to do all [build them up to maturity].This is the commission's kind of "evangelism" and "edification" which does not stop at conversion but makes spiritually mature disciples in Christ.

Christ's closing promise [by My Spirit]

This closing promise is transmitted by every generation of believers. In John 17:20, Christ prays,

*"I do not pray for these alone, but also for those **who will believe** in Me through your word"* Emphasis added.

Christ's promise of His presence, *"I am with you always,"* guarantees the success of the church's mission, because it is really His mission carried out by His called-out disciples. Therefore Christ's *empowerment* of the church through the Holy Spirit and the Word working in tandem are essential to evangelizing the world and is available in every generation, until the end of the church age.

The church is called to declare in word and demonstrate in deed the character of Christ who lives within His people.

In comparing the Great Commission with Jesus' promise to continually build His church; we conclude that Jesus undoubtedly intends for His church to be spiritually militant and evangelistically aggressive disciples who spread the gospel to the world of our generation:

"Behold I send the Promise of My Father upon you; but tarry in the city of Jerusalem until you are endued with power from on high" (Luke 24:49).

"But you shall receive power when the Holy Spirit has come upon you; and you shall be witnesses to Me in Jerusalem, and in Judea, and Samaria, and to the end of the earth" (Acts 1:8).

Jesus has employed a simple plan [2 Timothy 2:2] for the proper execution of His mandate which consists of three successive stages:

1. Each believer [disciple] is to be *personally* empowered by the Holy Spirit.
2. Each believer [disciple] once empowered by the Spirit is by his or her personal testimony to win *others* to Christ.
3. These *others* [disciples] (that are won and made) are in turn to be empowered by the Spirit and win yet *others*.

In this manner the testimony of Jesus is extended outward from Jerusalem in ever-widening circles of *power* until it has reached the end of the earth that is, until it has reached all nations and every creature.

This plan is both simple and workable. When it is properly applied, it always works. Think about that! His plan makes possible the evangelization of the entire world in any century in which the church puts the plan to work. There is a flurry of activities and plans geared toward alternatives, but please remember when Christ instituted His plan above – He left absolutely no room for an alternative plan!

The word *power* in the scriptural passages above is the word *dunamis,* in the Greek from which we get our words *dynamite, dynamo,* and *dynamic.* The implications provided by these three English derivative words lead to our words *forceful* and *explosive impact.*

Growth to Maturity

God wants us to grow to spiritual maturity and fulfill His intended purpose in us. You may be asking yourself, am I growing toward maturity? The shallowness of instructions and orientation upon entering many churches today has new Christians and many older Christians as well asking this question. It should be understood at the outset, spiritual growth does not come as a result of your trying.

In order to grow we must first insure that those things necessary for proper spiritual growth are present. The apostle Paul put forth in his

Ephesians 4:13-16 the ultimate goal of the life of faith; and way of our assurance that we are growing to God's goal of spiritual maturity. He admonishes that God's goal for us is to,

"Attain to the unity of the faith and of the knowledge of the Son of God to mature manhood," to the measure of the stature of the fullness of Christ; so that we may no longer be children, tossed to and fro and carried about with every wind of doctrine, by the cunning of men, by their craftiness in deceitful wiles. Rather, speaking the truth in love, we are to grow up in every way into him who is the head, into Christ, from whom the whole body, joined and knit together by every joint with which it is supplied, when each part is working properly, makes bodily growth and builds itself in love" (Ephesians 4:13-16). Emphasis added.

If you are concerned about your personal growth toward maturity, please know, you cannot measure your progress by comparison with someone else. Instead, make sure the essentials necessary for growth are present in you. The apostle Paul concludes concerning spiritual growth to maturity in the following twofold way by increasing in:

1. The unity of the faith (correct doctrine)
2. The knowledge of the Son of God (experience)

He says these will lead to *mature manhood,* the measure of the stature of the fullness of Christ" (v. 13).

The unity of the faith

The unity of the faith is the church's shared understanding, of the *deeper truths* revealed in the Word of God. The Word of God is immutable [unchanging], the new light of knowledge of "these deeper truths" is continually manifesting forth from them through prophets and teachers by the Holy Spirit. Christians whether those just starting out or those who have journeyed a while grow when they strive and put forth much effort themselves to understand the unity of the faith. They gain the knowledge of the truth with the help of pastors, teachers and other leaders who make themselves available to them within the body of Christ. Absolutely no growth toward maturity [perfection] can occur without this *increase* in the unity of the faith through the understanding of Christian *doctrine* by the Holy Spirit.

However, it must also be accompanied by an *increase* in the knowledge of the Son of God. This refers to *experience,* with an initial and growing encounter with the Lord Jesus Christ Himself, so that we know Him directly and personally – this is the other essential that makes spiritual growth possible. This occurs when the knowledge of the faith is *learned* and put into practice [*doing*]. Just as the Spirit and the Word works in tandem, so does hearing and doing.

You will never know Jesus Christ without following Him!

To know Him is to love Him

The disciples had an acquaintance [knew of Him] with Jesus Christ before they became His disciples. But they never *knew* Him until they began to interact with Him and left all to follow Him.

Realizing that growth is a matter of knowledge and obedience, we should not be discouraged because we are not completely like Christ, but we realize we are His work in progress. The Scripture assures us, what He has begun He will finish!

Practical experience

In conjunction with Paul's admonition above, ask yourself:

- Have I moved away from childish things?
- Have I forsaken infantile attitudes and behavior?
- Am I governed by childish reactions and outbursts?

This is the first step in checking your maturity, the apostle Paul and other writers have much to say in exhorting us concerning childlikeness, but not childishness. Childishness and childlikeness are two different matters:

- Childlikeness – is the simple faith which believes God and acts accordingly.
- Childishness – is marked by instability and naiveté.

A childish Christian is marked by:

- A short attention span.
- He or she is unstable, tossed to and fro.
- Carried about by every changing circumstance.
- Eager to start new projects or ministry, but soon interests wane.
- Confident and arrogant.
- Think they are fall-proof.
- Peter's behavior in (Mark 14:29-30).

In his book *"Emotionally Healthy Spirituality,"* Peter Scazzero sheds light on another very important hindrance in our spiritual growth to maturity. Using the iceberg as an example, he walks us through an experience we all have. His thesis is that, most of us will admit that there are deep layers beneath our daily observances. Therefore, like an iceberg where only about 10 percent is visible above the surface; similarly this 10 percent represents the visible changes we make that are visible to others. We are more respectable, clean from alcohol and drugs, cursing, illicit behavior and the like. We attend church and participate regularly.

But the roots of who we are continue unaffected. The problem is the 90 percent of *me* is inward and out of sight [like the iceberg it's under water]; which remains untouched by Jesus Christ until there is a total renewal of the soul [mind, will, emotions]. Unless we humbly submit [the whole me] to the work of the Spirit and the Word working outwardly from our now born again spirit, this untouched access baggage [in the mind, will, or emotions] begins to solidify and hinder growth to maturity. We've all probably experienced that one person on the board or committee, who shout, "I've been this way all my life and I am not going to change! The point, it is impossible to be spiritually mature while remaining emotionally immature.[6]

The author concludes that by not paying attention to God and what is going on inside of you causes you to miss many gifts. Christ speaks [seeking to get us to change] but we are not listening [the author characterizes this as "emotionally unhealthy spirituality]. When the crisis comes it opens us to new truth that we have not been fully acknowledging. It is a great part of our life stuffed away in that 90 percent of me that is *held inside* under the surface. God made each of us a whole person, in His image (see Genesis 1:27).

Included in that image are physical, spiritual, emotional, intellectual, and social components. Ignoring any one component or aspect of who we are as an individual person made in God's image always results in destructive consequences – in our relationship with God, with others, and with ourselves.

Unlike looking upon someone with an obvious lack of mental or physical development is apparent. However, emotional underdevelopment is not so obvious having known a person only for a short period of time. It is sad to say that even in selecting some church officers including pastors have proven to have been unwise selections as characteristics begin emerging over a period of time from deep under the surface of that unseen 90 percent portion of the person that continually so neatly stuffed away now begins to emerge; and soon the Dr. Jekyll and Mr. Hyde personality appears [the real person].

Paul also warned the church concerning "novices." In Ephesians 5:18, we are commanded to "be filled with the Spirit!" Continuously "being filled" with the Spirit leaves no room for anything else. So let us walk so "in Christ." The first prerequisite of those first officers appointed in Acts 6 was that they ["be full of the Holy Spirit"]. The law of first mention would suggest that this is true for any and every position in the church [meaning no position is so insignificant that this can be overlooked.

CHAPTER 11: DISCUSSION

1. "Go" conveys the force of the command to
   _____ _____.

2. The 1ˢᵗ step is "_____" them.

3. The 2ⁿᵈ step is "_____ _____"

4. Discuss "being full of the Holy Spirit" and the church's success.

5. Discuss Jesus' promise to continually build His church.

6. Explain Jesus' simple plan of execution for the Great Commission.

7. The first step in checking your spiritual maturity is _____ which is simple faith that believes God and acts accordingly.

8. Define a novice; and explain Paul's concern abut them in reference to the church.

Chapter Twelve

SPIRITUALLY RADICAL

"Live in harmony with one another......Repay no one evil for evil .... Do not be overcome by evil, but overcome evil with good" (Romans 12:14, 21).

A major hindrance facing Christian leaders today is the growing desire for them and their churches to be popular and politically-correct throughout the culture and wider society rather than to be biblically obedient and faithful to God. Genuine leadership focuses on helping all of the people possible; and living a righteous Christlike life to the glory of God.

It takes great humility, deep conviction and a Spirit-filled life to be an effective church leader today. Those seeking the applause of the public by succumbing to their tastes and preferences are in reality disasters waiting to happen. Political correctness must never be allowed to displace biblical correctness. The churches in America for the most part have resigned themselves to existence through planned-programs focused and conducted for the most part within the four walls of the church building.

As more churches continue to drop-out of the public conversation; the American society is made more radically bold in their demands including the priority to stamp "out our religious freedoms." Many of these criticisms toward the Church of God go un-countered biblically by our pulpits. Due to spiritual and biblical ignorance in the churches more and more of the members are sympathizing and allowing themselves to be dumb-downed, overcome and controlled by up and down feelings and unbiblical politics; and therefore they arrive at the same secularist attitudes and conclusions as the humanistic culture – demanding that the church either agree with their progressive agenda or just be silent and blend in with us. However, the progressive agenda counter-opposes the church's biblically based opposition:

- The church opposes immorality in any form.
- The church opposes abortions.
- The church opposes cohabitation.
- The church has become too political.
- The church opposes same-sex marriages.
- The church has insisted that Jesus is the only way to God.
- The church is become bigoted and intolerant.
- The church's message is exclusive.
- The church is otherworldly – minded.
- The church says, "You must be born from above" to belong.
- The church is more interested in "what you are [character]" than "what you do [performance]."

Rather than take a stand as Spiritual radicals and respond by defending the biblical faith, principles, and practices, many churches are simply silent on the [sin] issues of today's society. As a result of this stance by the church the secular culture has become bolder in their ungodly demands against religious freedom.

The cry of the culture and media insisting that the church leave the public square to them and their secular worldviews have become more vocal against biblical truth and the foundational principles that has maintained the favor of God upon us all.

Pew Power

Research shows that about nine out of ten Christian pastors admit that they have retreated to the safety of their church properties and refuse to take up the battle to equip their people in the pews for spiritual warfare. It seems that as Christ stands at the door knocking that 1 out of 10 "hears" "and goes" out to meet Him in kingdom mission while the nine remain inside and silent. As I stated in an earlier section, evolution has been elevated up above Christianity in the public square – everything in media and education [from K – Ph D] is raised on this unproven lie!

- Think about it, we can no longer have prayer, Bible reading, religious gatherings, and moral teaching on our tax-paid public school premises.
- Millions of our school children are controlled by medication.
- Children are taught in school that they evolved from apes.
- Parents are prohibited from disciplining their children.
- The state has taken over marriage, defying God and His Word.
- Divorce can now be handled on line.
- Marriage and the family have been redefined.
- Our children are being taught that there is no absolute truth.
- Morally challenging sermons are considered "hate speech."
- The government has substituted policies and programs which have very subtly restricted parental guidance, and religious freedoms.
- America is no longer, "we the people" as the judicial branch overrides or passes down decisions that cannot be altered by the other branches of government.
- The entertainment industries produce material with the sole purpose of inflaming the lusts of adults, teens, and dull the consciousness of the general population.
- Jesus Christ is downgraded and removed from the public square, while Hollywood celebrities and many Christian TV personalities are being held up as worthy of worship.
- The biblical worldview is set aside and replaced with a variety of secular views based on feelings, technology, and erroneous interpretations of biblical truth.

The Failure of the Body

Church history reflects that the gospel germinated in a social climate similar to our own. It was a time of:

- Injustice
- Racial division
- Social unrest

- Rampant crime
- Gross immorality
- Economic uncertainty
- Widespread fear

The early Christian church struggled to survive under persecution so harsh it is beyond our imagination. They did not see their calling as one of fighting injustice and oppression, or demanding its "rights." The early church saw its mission as one of:

- *Reflecting God's holiness*
- *Revealing God's glory*
- *Witnessing to the reality of Christ*

The church did so by demonstrating unconditional love toward those within the church and those on the outside. Keep in mind our war is spiritual; therefore, true spiritual militant change in people is from the inside out. How the churches handle things at this point can send them astray. Christ came into the world to transform society, but He did not come to do so through political action.

Christ's plan was to change society by transforming the individual people in the society!

A New Heart

Christ planned to accomplish this by giving them a new birth in the spirit, a new heart, through a cleansing and new orientation [renewed soul] on life, a resurrection life, and the death of self. Once individuals are transformed they become part of a new society:

- "We are changed from within; the inside is cleansed and our outlook on human relationships changes.
- We are changed; therefore when we are confronted with mistreatment – our *natural* reflex is to respond with "an eye for

an eye." But Jesus has called us to a new kind of response – "Bless those who persecute you."

- We are changed, so the response of the apostle Paul for us becomes, "Live in harmony with one another......... Repay no one evil for evil ..... Do not be overcome by evil, but overcome evil with good" (Romans 12:14-21).

Lest we forget

We are changed (see 2 Corinthians 5:17), and as the church we are to effect radical spiritual change in people. The false religion, secular humanism, and the culture are here to oppose us. If we are not careful, the church may find itself actually made to feel vulnerable by threats from government and special interest groups against those not agreeing to promote their agenda. To assimilate many church leaders are bending and blending God's moral laws to conform. Through spiritual and biblical ignorance Christians corporately and individually are deviating from the *revealed truths* of God's eternal Word.

Secular humanism has denied all earlier claims of being a religion in order to promote humanity to a place above their Creator, God. No longer considering themselves a religion they openly deny the very existence of the Holy Trinity [God the Father, Jesus Christ the Son, and the Holy Spirit]. Therefore, to them man is the measure of all things.

We mere humans cannot improve on God's divine plan. Nor are we left in doubt as to what that calling is. In the Book of Ephesians, the first three chapters are devoted to describing that call, and it is also detailed elsewhere in the New Testament. If we are to intelligently obey our Lord; we must give the highest priority to understanding what He wants us to be and to do.

We exist to reflect God's holiness, to reveal His glory, and witness to the fact that Jesus has come to save and cleanse people from the inside out. We exist to love one another, and to radically demonstrate Christlike love and character to the world through obedience and living a righteous life before them. That is our purpose. That is our calling!

Practice Patience

In clearly knowing our purpose and calling, it is imperative that the church be patient and forbearing, knowing the seeds of truth takes time to grow into a full harvest. We are to be careful to not demand that society suddenly change long established social patterns. At the same time the church is to effect positive change by having no part with evil; but practice righteous living, thus planting seeds of truth to take root in society; which ultimately will produce the fruit of change.

Some carnal Christians in our midst would say this strategy is frivolous, however a check of Church history reflects; this is exactly the Spirit-led strategy that upset the Roman Empire as the church carried the gospel to the ends of the earth. Period historians wrote that "the little group of saints had turned the world upside down." Christlike Christian love brought the Empire to its knees. Christian love was unstoppable then and can be just as unstoppable in America today if we would only repent and return to God.

A unifying Force

The supreme mark of the true child of God as stated by Christ Himself is love. Love that:

- is unconditional
- accepts others as they are
- kindhearted and forgiving
- seeks to heal misunderstanding and division
- seeks to mend broken relationships
- seeks to meet needs

Jesus said, *"By this all men will know that you are My disciples, if you have love for one another"* (John 13:35). This love that Jesus advocates is never manifested by the ways of the world:

- greed
- rivalry
- indifference
- jealousy

- envy
- pride
- prejudice
- division

Christlike Christian love, *the unifying force*, enables the church [not the general populace] through the Holy Spirit to carry out its mission in the world. We must never forget the culture war is a spiritual war between good and evil [hate and love] already won by the love of God (see John 3:16):

> *"For God so loved the world*
> *that He gave His only begotten Son,*
> *that whosoever believes on Him should not perish,*
> *but have everlasting life."*

The Battle Cry

- We are to reflect God's holiness.
- We are to reveal God's glory.
- We are to witness to the reality of Jesus Christ.

Our risen Lord and Savior Jesus Christ came among us to implant within us His own everlasting life. That is the message of hope and love that we must radically bring to a hostile and fearful world. This is the calling of the church. This is the "Battle Cry" of the true church today!

Have we reached the end?

Nearly two thousand years ago the Apostle Paul wrote a letter to a young pastor named Timothy. In that letter 2 Timothy 3:1-5 he explains how Christians will be conquered in the last days and marked by gross sin. **"But know this, that in the last days perilous times will come. For men (people) will be:**

- Lovers of themselves
- Lovers of money
- Boasters

- Proud
- Blasphemers
- Disobedient to parents
- Unthankful
- Unholy
- Immoral
- Without love
- Unforgiving
- Slanderous
- Without self-control
- Brutal
- Not lovers of the good
- Traitors
- Headstrong
- Haughty
- Lovers of pleasure rather than lovers of God
- Having a form of godliness, but denying the power thereof.

Paul advises the church to "have nothing to do with them" (see II Timothy 3:1-5). We invite people to come to Jesus as they are however; they are not to remain just as they are. Why? Simply because the characteristics he saw (listed above) would consume the church if allowed to run rampart without being challenged.

Reading Paul's words written nearly two thousand years ago sounds as if he was looking down through the ages at present day America. Dr. Billy Graham commenting on this condition is reported to have said, "It means we have allowed Christians to possess these characteristics mainly through assimilation by allowing them to remain in the Christian Community. Many of these people have no intention of changing; clearly showing Satan's footprints are clearly visible.

Chapter 12: DISCUSSION

1. According to this writer, to be an effective leader it takes a deep commitment, a great humility and a _____ _____ life.

2. Discuss the problems causing many churches to withdraw from the public square.

3. Has the church in America become too liberal and political?

4. Contrast the culture in which the early churches of the first century existed with our culture today.

5. As the true church we are to _____ _____ _____.

6. Christ strategy to change a society is one individual at a time. Is that the churches' strategy today?

7. Christian love was unstoppable in the early church – what is it like today in our churches?

8. Discuss Paul's explanation for Christians being conquered by the world.

Chapter Thirteen

THE FINAL GOAL: MATURITY

We come now to Paul's statement of the supreme goal of all of God's strategy for humanity. God's goal says Paul is:

"Till we all come into the unity of the faith and of the knowledge of the Son of God, to a perfect man, to the measure of the stature of the fullness of Christ; that we should no longer be children, tossed to and fro and carried about with every wind of doctrine, by the trickery of men, in the cunning craftiness of deceitful plotting, but speaking the truth in love, may grow up in all things into Him who is the head – Christ – from whom the whole body, joined and knit together by what every joint supplies, according to the effective working by which every part does its share, causes growth of the body for the edifying of itself in love" (Ephesians 4:13-16).

On two occasions in this flagship passage, the apostle Paul gives us the supreme goal of *the life of faith*. It is the standard measure by which we can judge our progress as Christians. Notice he said it is:

1. "The measure of the stature of the fullness of Christ" (v. 13).
2. "To grow up in all things into Him who is the Head – Christ" (v. 15).

We see that God wants us to fulfill our humanity – which He intended when He created Adam and Eve. It is also clear in this passage that the supreme goal of the church is evangelization of the world. Jesus has clearly sent us [corporately] to preach the gospel of the kingdom to every creature. However, God's ultimate goal for each believer [individually] is that we be *"conformed to the image of His Son"* Evangelization is the means of bringing people from all walks of life into a right relationship with God and fulfill His ultimate goal for them – Christlikeness. And that is what the church is all about. It is God's instrument:

- To achieve mature humanity – a humanity exactly like that which was characterized by the life of Jesus Christ.
- Producing men and women who demonstrate the character qualities of Jesus Christ.

We have seen the full plan, and we are now back where the apostle Paul began: the church is to fulfill its calling – of demonstrating to the world a new character, "in Christ" with a:

- spirit of meekness
- love and unity
- resurrection power

This proves that the church is a body of true Christ-followers who are empowered by the Holy Spirit directed by God Himself.

Christian Maturity

Today maturity seems to be in the eyes of the beholder in our churches. One might say this person is mature or that person is immature, but by what standards are these conclusions reached? If you think this way, you can see that maturity must be considered relative and up to the individual.

The truth of the matter is, the only true objective standard for Christian maturity is Christ Himself. Research after research has shown that Bible reading in this country is spiraling downward daily. As a result much of what is believed by many Christians is mere hearsay of 2nd or 3rd hand information circulating among Christians in general. So when we use the term "mature" our limited knowledge is imperfect; and as a result we end up many times comparing ourselves with others – as we see it.

In 1 John 2:12, the apostle John gives us a helpful way to see maturity as various progressive levels of our spiritual and biblical growth to maturity. We should understand that John is not talking about the physical or biological age here, but where we are or should be in our various levels of spiritual growth to being a mature disciple of Christ. He writes,

> *"I write to you, dear children,*
> *because your sins are forgiven*
> *through Christ.*
> *I write to you, parents,*
> *because you know the One who existed*
> *from the beginning.*
> *I write to you, young people,*
> *because you have defeated the*
> *evil one.*
> *I write to you, children,*
> *because you know the Father.*
> *I write to you parents,*
> *because you know the One who existed*
> *from the beginning.*
> *I write to you, young people,*
> *because you are strong;*
> *the teaching of God lives in you,*
> *and you have defeated the evil one.*
> *— 1 John 2:12-14 NEV*

Level one of maturity

John classified this first group as "little children" as they are glorifying God and celebrating the fact that in their understanding He has forgiven their sins. This does not mean they are mature – but this marks the initial or level one of their spiritual and biblical growth toward Christian maturity and discipleship.

Level two of maturity

He addresses the second group as "parents" because you *know* Him [Jesus Christ] who is from the beginning. The mark of a spiritual parent then is one possessing a deep and biblical experiential understanding of the deity and the humanity of Jesus -- with fullness of the biblical knowledge and fellowship with Him throughout much of life.

This level of maturity displays an understanding and a manifestation of the same character that Jesus consistently manifested along with the evidence of:

- Love
- Compassion
- Tolerance
- Patience
- Justice
- Forgiveness

This "fruit," is produced as the results of a long term relationship with the Son of God.

The final level

Lastly, he addresses the "young people," who are characterized as having *overcome the evil one,* after having reached a level of maturity and [sanctification] where there is an understanding and a practice of the way to handle temptation. Temptation comes from the devil and the ability to handle it is a mark of a mature Spirit-filled person of discernment [one who knows how to distinguish between good and evil].

They are functional and useful to the kingdom of God. This passage of Scripture makes it clear, the process of spiritual and biblical growth to Christian maturity does not happen all at once.

The writer of Hebrews put it this way,

"Solid food is for the mature, for those who have their faculties <u>*trained*</u> *by practice to distinguish good from evil"* (Hebrews 5:14).

The beloved apostle adds more emphasis by repeating these levels, while adding a few statements to the "children," "parents," and "young people" (again review 1 John 2:12-14).

How do you grow up?

Going back now to Paul and Ephesians 4, in verse 15, He admonishes, "We are to grow up in every way …… into Christ." In verse 16, he says the body "makes bodily growth and builds up itself in *love.*" Growth is God's method and His way. This principle is very crucial to understand:

- Many are disturbed after becoming Christians they don't find themselves instantly transformed into great super saints.
- They find much of the old life [sin nature] is still around.
- The old attitudes are still controlling their behavior,
- They don't know how to handle all of this, and many are tempted to believe they are not truly saved.
- They need to understand, if their faith is in Christ and His finished work – just walk in it!

They must be taught that there is a process of spiritual and biblical growth which must follow and it takes time to grow. Well just how is this done? The church must nurture their new Christians and insure that they learn the scriptural factors that enhance and encourages growth. These aids to growth must be present and ready for implementation.

Once they are properly put into place immediately growth will occur itself, without force. As we discussed in an earlier section, the apostle Paul gives a twofold way:

1. Increasing in "the unity of the faith." [Which is the shared understanding of the great truths revealed in the scriptures in the church].
2. Increasing in the knowledge of the Son of God." [Here he refers to experienceing, a growing encounter with the Lord Jesus Christ Himself, so that we can come to know Him more and more – not just know about Him. Know Him personally!

This personal encounter occurs when the knowledge of the truth through (hearing) is put into practice (doing). The three synoptic gospels witness to the fact that the disciples had an acquaintance with Jesus [they knew of Him], but they never [knew Him] *until* they left all and followed Him. It is crucial at this point that the new Christians have the sincere prayers and concerns of the other members of the body. These he says, will lead to full maturity,

> *"Until we all reach unity*
> *in the faith*
> *and in the knowledge*
> *of*
> *the Son of God*
> *and become mature*
> *attaining*
> *the measure of the stature*
> *of*
> *the fullness of Christ."*
>
> – Ephesians 4:13

Unity is not just a matter of a loving attitude or religious feeling, but of truth and a common understanding about God's Son; and the maturity of the perfectly balanced character of Christ.

Chapter 13: DISCUSSION

1. According to Paul, the supreme goal of God's plan for humanity is _____ of the _____.

2. God expects us to fulfill our humanity as we are _____ to the image of _____ _____.

3. Discuss the church's call of demonstrating to the world a new character "in Christ."

4. Discuss the only true objective standard for Christian character is _____ _____.

5. According to this chapter, the mark of a spiritual parent are:
   a.
   b.
   c.

6. The Christian who with discernment has the ability to distinguish between good and evil.

7. Discuss the Christian's growing experience after their personal encounter with Christ.

8. Discuss the disciples knowing Christ personally and then knowing of Him. What incident recorded in all three of the synoptic gospels made clear the fact that they knew Him personally?

Chapter Fourteen

A WITNESS

"You will receive power when the Holy Ghost comes upon you" (Acts 1:8).

In the late 60's while stationed at Fort Knox, Kentucky my family and I joined the Morning Star Missionary Baptist Church in Vine Grove, Kentucky. Our pastor taught classes on evangelism to the whole church, and then instituted a weekly commitment to go out two by two and "evangelize" in the town from 6:00-8:00 PM; afterward we would assemble back at the church and share our experiences.

My wife and I learned a great deal about sharing our faith during those months; which proved to be Spirit-led as we were blessed to institute evangelism ministries at duty stations in the United States and overseas over the next two decades while serving in the U.S. Army. We had the privilege of helping to lead many people to saving faith in Christ.

During a two year tour of duty in Seoul, Korea, my wife and several of the other ladies in our fellowship taught English too many Korean National students, using the Bible, itself for a textbook. I accepted the call into the gospel ministry a couple of months after we arrived in Korea. Working closely with the Chaplains, the Church of God Servicemen's Center and local missionaries many souls were saved, soldiers and civilians alike. To God goes all the glory! Earlier in our ministry like many others we taught and practiced "Evangelism Explosion."[7]

The Holy Spirit [out and in] Evangelism

Over the past several decades many churches have forfeited their God-given mandate to evangelize the world for Christ. Even in denominations, evangelism seems to be optional among their churches. I personally believe the churches for the most part have programmed and organized themselves out of a viable witnessing opportunity.

For too many churches today evangelism happens at the end of the Sunday morning services' invitation to discipleship and that extended within the four walls only. I've heard some pastors bragging of their ten to fifteen minute sermonettes, show choirs, and dancers; with all of it timed and programed? As I stated in an earlier section many have divorced the Holy Spirit and His ministries. That is a sad commentary for none can come to the Lord *except* the Spirit draws them.

One thing is clear: We can't experience Christ's transforming power and joy for life *without* being filled with the Holy Spirit and under the control of Jesus, our Lord and Savior (see Ephesians 5:18-20).

The Power of Evangelism

Many churches turn to Acts 1:8 for the foundation of the challenge to express themselves as witnesses of Christ's good news. Prior to the Ascension mandate, Jesus promised *power* [pratos] from the Holy Spirit to be with His witnesses in Jerusalem, Judea, Samaria, and to the ends of the earth.

In reading this commission most put the major emphasis on "be My *witnesses*." For those of us interested in the Pentecostal persuasion our focus is on the integration *power* of the Holy Spirit in the witness. Again as He said, "You will receive power when the Holy Spirit comes on you." This misplacing of priorities has cost many to believe evangelism is extinct.

The Holy Spirit is still the unknown member of the Trinity in many Christian Communities. Others only experience the Holy Spirit in the miraculous. Then there are those who say His work ended at Pentecost.

The Holy Spirit's work is neither silent nor absent. He has many roles in the lives of Christians and the corporate body. I will name several:

- He gives us Spiritual gifts severely as He wills (see 1Corinthians 12; Romans 12; Ephesians 4).
- He cultivates our character (see Galatians 5:22, 23).
- He reveals and teaches us the truth (see John 14:16).
- He gives us power to be witnesses (see Acts 1.8).

This sets the foundation for walking in the Spirit and demonstrating the fruit of the Spirit (see Galatians 5:22, 23).

Fit for Service

Today millions of people the world over are frustrated with politicians, poverty, pain, suffering and injustice. The work of the church should be directed toward this desperate world. By Christ's command every member is required to step forward for service to accomplish the mission at hand. However, to do this everyone has to be spiritually fit, that is with *resurrection power* our zeal for witness overflows.

The church suffers great damage today by worship that has become dull, without spirit and totally predictable. Sadly many have more reverence for their traditions and programs than *biblical truth.* The results produced are *soulish* not *spiritual.* Christian love and fellowship are superficial resulting in very little real involvement in each other's lives. The true warm fellowship among Christians which the New Testament calls *koinonia,* was an essential part of early Christianity and remains so to this day.

Christian Love

The New Testament puts heavy responsibility upon Christians to *know* each other close enough to be able to gather together for instruction, to study and pray together, share their spiritual gifts, bear one another's burdens, confess faults one to another, and minister to one another with the Word of God, song and prayer.

Then guided by the Holy Spirit and the Word of God they would go out into the world to let their fruit of the Spirit manifest in love-filled lives – drawing the unsaved into the church. This was precisely what Jesus meant with the exhortation to His disciples:

"A new commandment I give you that you love one another; even as I have loved you that you also love one another. By this all men will know that you are My disciples, if you have love for one another" (John 13:34-35).

The New Testament has some fifty or more of these ministry commands recorded calling us to a special kind of life together.
Listed in the NIV are:

- "Be at peace with each other" (Mark 9:50).
- "Wash one another's feet" (John 13:14).
- "Love one another" (John 13:34).
- "Love one another" (John 13:35).
- "Love each other" (John 15:12).
- "Love each other" (John 15:17).
- "Be devoted to one another in brotherly love" (Romans 12:10).
- "Honor one another above yourself" (Romans 12:10).
- "Live in harmony with one another" (Romans 12:16).
- "Love one another" (Romans 13:8).
- "Accept one another, then, just as Christ accepted you" (Romans 15:7).
- "Instruct one another" (Romans 15:14).
- "Greet one another with a holy kiss" (Romans 16:16).
- "When you come together to eat, wait for each other" (1 Corinthians 11:33).
- "Have equal concern for each other" (1 Corinthians 12:25).
- "Greet one another with a holy kiss" (2 Corinthians 13:12).
- "Serve one another in love" (Galatians 5:13).
- "If you keep on biting and devouring one another … you will be destroyed by each other" (Galatians 5:26).
- "Let us not become conceited, provoking and envying each other" (Galatians 5:15).
- "Carry each other's burdens" (Galatians 6:2).
- "Be patient, bearing with one another in love" (Ephesians 4:32).
- "Be kind and compassionate to one another" (Ephesians 4:32).
- "Forgiving each other" (Ephesians 4:32).

- "Speak tone another with psalms, hymns, and spiritual songs" (Ephesians 5:19).
- "Submit to one another out of reverence for Christ" (Ephesians 5:21).
- "In humility consider others better than yourselves" (Philippians 2:3).
- "Do not lie to each other" (Colossians 3:9).
- "Bear with each other" (Colossians 3:13).
- "Forgive whatever grievances you may have against one another" (Colossians 3:13).
- "Teach [one another]" (Colossians 3:16).
- "Admonish one another" (Colossians 3:16).
- "Make your love increase and overflow for each other" (1 Thessalonians 3:12).
- "Love each other" (1 Thessalonians 4:9).
- "Encourage each other" (1 Thessalonians 4:18).
- "Encourage one another" (1 Thessalonians 5:11).
- "Build each other up" (1 Thessalonians 5:11).
- "Encourage one another daily" (Hebrews 3:113).
- "Spur one another on toward love and good deeds" (Hebrews 10:24).
- "Encourage one another" (Hebrews 10:25).
- "Do not slander one another" (James 4:11).
- "Don't grumble against each other" (James 5:9).
- "Confess your sins to each other" (James 5:16).
- "Love one another deeply, from the heart" (1 Peter 1:22).
- "Live in harmony with one another"(1 Peter 3:8).
- "Love each other deeply" (1 Peter 4:8).
- "Offer hospitality to one another without grumbling" (1 Peter 4:9).
- "Each should use whatever gift he has received to serve others" (1 Peter 4:10).
- Clothe yourself with humility toward one another" (1 Peter 5:5).
- Greet one another with a kiss of love" (1 Peter 5:14).
- "Love one another" (1 John 3:11).
- "Love one another" (1 John 3:23).
- "Love one another" (1 John 4:7).
- "Love one another" (1 John 4:11).

- "Love one another" (1 John 4:12).
- "Love one another" (2 John 5).

It is quite apparent that these ministries in the body of Christ are important to God, since He repeated them over and over again in His Word. What provisions are made by pastors and other church leaders to encourage these ministries?

Corporate Cleansing

Before I retired from the Army, I would come home in the evening after having been amongst smokers all day at work, the smell of smoke lingered on me. When we spend time in the world, it inevitably gets on us – like the lingering smell of cigarette smoke.

If we avoid fellowshipping with other Christians for long periods of time and associate only with our non-Christian friends and co-workers, we start thinking about off-colored jokes, we've heard, or if not careful fall prey to coveting after the same material possessions that they covet.

If the situation is not corrected soon – I will become like the people I'm hanging around!

If I'm in the world (and as Jesus' disciple I am certainly supposed to be), I get the world on me. That's why it's so imperative that I come regularly to the gathering of fellow Christians. I have often heard people say that they go church for a refill. I like that but I would further say it's like filling an air conditioner with refrigerant before you can fill it – you must purge the system of all the old contaminates. Christian fellowship is where I confess my sins and re-align my priorities with the priorities of God.

Located in the outer court of the tabernacle was a large basin of water. The priests were commanded by God to wash their hands and feet before entering the holy place of prayer and worship. The idea here in the brazen laver [basin] was to wash [cleanse] (*water here parallels the Word of God* which cleanses us). Looking into the Word has a mirror affect. We see ourselves repent and confess, [take care of the daily defilement picked will walking in the world].

A three-fold witness

The early church relied upon a three-fold witness as their means of reaching a paganized and cynical an unbelieving world:

- *Kerugma* – proclamation by a herald[8]
- *Didache* – teaching, doctrine, instruction[9]
- *Koinonia* – communion, fellowship[10]

The deep love and concern early Christians had for one another and the way they shared their lives with each other in the church – left the pagan world interested in "koinonia." One pagan writer remarked, "How these Christians love one another!"

In spite of the successes with these main ingredients essential for an effective early church; it is very sad that many churches today have chosen to do away with the didache [teaching] and koinonia [fellowship] completely leaving only the kerygma [proclamation]. In doing so, the church has removed God's provision and protective guardrails from around the church's health [holiness] and greatly reduced and weakened its witness to the world making the church irrelevant to many people in the world.

Restoring Koinonia

It is significant that church history reports whenever spiritual awakenings have occurred, they have been accompanied by a restoration of koinonia fellowship which includes confession of faults and bearing of one another's burdens. This kind of ministry in the church greatly reduces much of the pastors' and other church leaders' counseling and crisis intervention. Christian love and concern for the brothers and sisters in the church reduces many spiritual, emotional, and even some mental problems. Christians should be equipped and experientially-prepared to share the heavy burdens of other brothers and sisters.

It has been said, "Had there not been a Barnabas [son of encouragement] there would never have been a Paul. Those with the gift of encouragement should be used mightily for the kingdom in ministry with those who are downcast, appear troubled and withdrawn. A listening ear accompanies the gift of encouragement.

The church's scriptural mission of building up and edifying one another is "speaking the truth in love" (see Ephesians 4:15). This word "speaking" carries with it a sense not only of speaking the truth but demonstrating the truth through every area of our lives. The problem is though most of us don't want to speak, especially in confrontation. Confrontation is an area where Christians often fail one another – which allows church to become much less effective in witness.

When we remain silent in these matters we do that person a great injustice. We actually condemn them to go on hurting others, suffering rejection, when we could allow the Spirit to use us to produce positive change in him or her. We convince ourselves that our cowardice action is actually an act of "Christian love."

Christians who have experienced true koinania can tell you they are grateful beyond words that another Christian has cared enough to help them become more mature and more like Jesus Christ. This is the ministry of washing one another's feet, which Jesus said was absolutely necessary among His disciples:

"If I then, your Lord and Teacher, having washed your feet, you also ought to wash one another's feet. For I have given you an example that you also should do as I have done unto you" (John 13:14-15).

Taken symbolically what Jesus said is seen literally in what He said,
"What I am doing you do not know now, but afterward you will understand" (John 13:7).

It is not too difficult to keep a church healthy and alive, providing the leadership and members alike are diligent to bear one another's burdens, to teach and practice repentance and confession of our faults one to another, instruct one another, and admonish one another in love. As we do so we enable the church to be all that God meant it to be doctrinally and experiential pure: "a church without spot or wrinkle or any such thing" (Ephesians 5:27).

CHAPTER 14: DISCUSSION

1. Discuss the church's commitment to witness for the Lord.

2. How is the absence of the Holy Spirit and His ministry affecting the local church?

3. Discuss the renewal of "koinania" in our churches today.

4. Discuss the 3-fold witness approach of the early church. Would its implementation help the church today?

5. Discuss how the implementation of the "One another" ministry could help in today's local churches.

6. Discuss the effects on the many churches today who have chosen to do away with the didache [teaching] and koinonia [fellowship] completely leaving only the kerygma [proclamation].

7. Why do so many Christians have problems in the area of confrontation in witnessing?

8. Define and discuss Christian fellowship.

Chapter Fifteen

THE URGENCY OF THE GOSPEL

Be diligent to present yourself unto God, a worker who does not need to be ashamed, rightly dividing the word of truth (2 Timothy 2:15).

The one piece of spiritual armor that God has placed to be viewed by the natural eye is His Word, the Holy Bible [*logos*]. The Bible has been translated into hundreds of languages and dialects. In the various languages, God gives human beings the ability to seek Him, find Him and to know Him. Before Jesus ascended back to heaven, He promised His disciples that the Father would send the Spirit of Truth to lead and guide us into all truth and understanding (study John 14-16).

The Spirit has given us a picture in the Word. The eunuch and Phillip are a good example of the importance and urgency of the gospel to God. He pulled Philip out of one of the greatest revivals recorded in the Bible to *help* this man understand and receive the true gospel of Christ. Satan knows the full potential and threat of Christians who are not only full of the Spirit, but full of God's Word as well. Therefore, one of his favorite deceptions is to lead people to believe that they can have a spiritual experience with God without His Word. We must remember, Jesus said His Word is Spirit and it is life. His Word is alive!

The Natural – then the Spiritual

The Word of God can be divided into two divisions the *natural* and the *spiritual:*

1. The natural division consists of the historical facts and the literal interpretation as recorded in the Bible.
2. The spiritual division consists of the Spiritual revelation knowledge of the truth and the fulfillment in the person of Jesus Christ and His Church.

The literal meaning is easy to see and understand, but the revelation truth is deeper and often more hidden.

For My thoughts are not your thoughts, neither are your ways My ways, says the Lord. For as the heavens are higher than the earth, so are My ways higher than your ways, and My thoughts than your thoughts (Isaiah 55:8-9).

Isaiah said that God does not think like us. Therefore, we cannot just casually read His Word and still understand what He meant when wrote it. Jesus said that the heavenly Father, *".... Hid these things from the wise and prudent ..... and revealed them unto babes ...."* (Like 10:21). Consider this:

- We cannot find something that God hid without God Himself *revealing* where He hid it.
- John said, *"A man [or woman] can receive nothing, except it be given him [or her] from heaven"* (John 3:27).
- It is wise to pray for the *"spirit of wisdom and revelation"* to get His help to finding the truth (Ephesians 1:17).

> *Open Thou mine eyes,*
> *That I may behold*
> *Wondrous things*
> *Out of Thy law*
>
> – Psalm 119:18 KJV

The Scriptures were written by men under the inspiration of the Holy Spirit (see 2 Timothy 3:16). There was a spiritual purpose in what they wrote, even when they simply recorded historical events. However, only those facts and events that were *relevant* to the spiritual truth that God wanted us to receive were recorded. That's why there are so many unanswered questions concerning what is recorded. An example of this is recorded in (see Genesis 4:17):

- Many people wonder where Cain's bride came from.
- Whose daughter was she?

God did not bother clarifying this for us because it would not have *revealed* anything of eternal value. That was not spiritually important, so He left it out. God's Word was not written to satisfy our curiosity, but it contains *"All things that pertain unto life and godliness"* (see 2 Peter 1:3).

"All Scripture is given by inspiration of God, and is profitable for doctrine, for reproof, for correction, for instruction in righteousness" (see 2 Timothy 3:16).

The apostle Paul adds, *"But the natural man does not receive the things of the Spirit of God; for they are foolishness to him: neither can he know them, because they are spiritually discerned"* (1 Corinthians 2:14).

Carnal-minded people cannot understand *revealed spiritual truth,* because it is divinely inspired and its primary purpose is to reveal spiritual truth. When the "intellects" take God's Word and attempt to interpret it based on their natural learning error is inevitable. At the same time, those who absolutely refuse to incorporate what God did write into their doctrinal understanding or leave out parts for convenience make equal error.

"For I testify unto every man that hears the words of the prophecy of this book, If any man shall add unto these things, God shall add unto him the plagues that are written in this book: And if any man shall take away from the words of this book of the prophecy, God shall take away his part out of the book of life, and out of the holy city, and from the things which are written in this book" (Revelation 22:18-19).

Camouflaged spiritual truth

Spiritual truth is often embedded or naturally covered with a camouflaged disguise. When we look closely behind the natural covering, we find the true truth. The Scripture says,

"Howbeit that was not first which is spiritual, but that which is natural; and afterward that which is spiritual" (1 Corinthians 15:46) John said, *"the Word was made flesh ......"* (John 1:14).

Before you can get to the grain, the natural husk of the corn must be peeled away. Jesus demonstrated the spirit of the Law rather than the letter of the Law. You have to look beyond His flesh and see His heart to see the Spiritual truth He embodied. Like so many in our churches today, the Jews were unable to see the Spiritual truth – they only saw the outer natural covering (see Matthew 13:53-57).

Jesus said, *"It is the Spirit who gives life;* **the flesh profits nothing:** *the words that I speak to you are spirit, and they are life"* (John 6:63). Emphasis added.

The Law is spiritual

When taking the truths revealed in the New Testament by Jesus and the apostles, and using them to unfold the secrets of the Old Testament – the results is a treasure-trove of available truth through prophecies and types for those who prayerfully search them out.

The Old Testament is the New Testament concealed – and the New Testament is the Old Testament revealed.

For example, in the Law Moses wrote, *"You shall not muzzle an ox while it treads out the grains"* (Deuteronomy 25:4).

Paul quoted the Law, *"You shall not muzzle the ox while it treads out the grains."* Then he continues, *is it the oxen God is concerned about?* Or does He say it altogether for our sakes? For our sakes no doubt, this is written, that he who plows should plow in hope, and he who threshes in hope should be partaker of his hope. If we have sown spiritual things for you, is it a great thing if we reap your material things? (1 Corinthians 9:9-11).

Even so the Lord has commanded that those who preach the gospel should live from the gospel" (v. 14).

Here Paul looked at the *natural* process of feeding oxen while they worked and applied that principle to the *support* of God's laborers. Paul referred to the spiritual meaning of Moses's commandment. Notice, the oxen symbolized God's ministers:

- The letter of the Law appeared to show *concern* for the oxen.
- But the spirit of the Law *reveled* God's *concern* for His laborers.

A Smorgasbord of the gospel

Many teachers today simply teach the law literally without seeking any spiritual truth. Others make a smorgasbord of the gospel of Christ, by attempting to mix law and grace; it's like trying to mix oil and water. The dress code for worship services seems to be a stickler today, and I will say a great hindrance to worship. The whole thing goes from requiring men to wear coats and ties to women not to wear pants. Notice the laws:

"Women shall not wear that which pertains to man, neither shall a man put on a woman's garment; for all that do so are abomination unto the Lord" (Deuteronomy 22:5).

The Scripture also says, *"...... the Lord sees not as man sees; for man looks on the outward appearance, but the Lord looks on the heart"* (1 Samuel 16:7).

The apostle Paul gave the *spiritual meaning* Moses' commandment:

"Do you not know that the unrighteous will not inherit the kingdom of God? Do not be deceived. Neither fornicators, nor idolaters, nor adulterers, nor

effeminate, abusers of themselves   will inherit the kingdom of God" (see 1 Corinthians 6:9).

Paul wrote this letter to the Church; Christians are agents of God called to influence and carry the light of Jesus Christ into a dark world. Rather than outward appearance he is addressing a heart thing. *Masculine* women and *effeminate* men are an abomination to God; and heading down a path that leads from God's design.

It's not our outside garments, *but the inner spiritual garments* we wear that God is concerned about. In Romans 13:14, Paul gives the *spiritual* dress code, *"But put on the Lord Jesus Christ, and make no provision for the flesh, to fulfill its lusts."*

Those who are clothed with the character of Christ, the fruit of the Spirit are well-dressed to God. Those who are clothed with their own works are naked and an abomination before Him *"...... for by the works of the law shall no flesh be justified."* (Galatians 2:16).

The Law and the Church

The overarching question is what part of the law still pertains to the church? Again, we turn to God's Word. When "certain men which came down [to Antioch] from Judea taught the brethren, and said, except you be circumcised after the manner of Moses, you cannot be saved" (see Acts 15:1), the church sent Paul and Barnabas to the apostles in Jerusalem. I think the church today should very well take heed to the results of this meeting or we might find ourselves caught up in the *curse* of Galatians 1:8-Listen to the Apostles counsel:

And they wrote letters ... unto the brethren which are of the Gentiles ... Forasmuch as we have heard, that certain which went out from us have troubled you with words, subverting your souls, saying, You must be circumcised, and keep the laws to whom we give no such commandment: It seems seemed good unto us, being assembled with one accord, to send chosen men unto you with our beloved Barnabas and Paul ... **For it seemed good to the Holy Ghost, and to us, to lay upon you no greater burden than these necessary things;** *That you abstain from meats offered to idols, and from blood, and from things strangled, and from fornication: from which if* *you keep yourselves, you shall do well* ... (Acts 15:23-29). Emphasis added throughout.

Jesus paid it all in His life and death, as He satisfied the righteous requirements of the law:

He has made alive together with Him, having forgiven you all trespasses, ***having wiped out the handwriting of requirements that was against us,*** *which was contrary to us. And He has taken it out of the way, having nailed it to the cross* (see Colossians 2:14).

Sin shall not have dominion over you, for you are not under law but under grace (Romans 6:14).

The law of the Spirit of life in Christ Jesus has made me free from the law of sin and death (Romans 8:2).

As I stated earlier, law and grace will not mix. When the law is sown into a person's heart, the fruit it bears is bondage and death; conversely, when God's grace is planted, it brings forth life and peace.

> ***For now we see***
> ***in a mirror,***
> ***dimly, but then***
> ***I shall know***
> ***just as I***
> ***also***
> ***am known.***

— 1 Corinthians 13:12

CHAPTER 15: DISCUSSION

1. When Jesus came He brought _____ and _____.

2. Discuss how revelation truth is deeper and hidden in the Word of God.

3. The Scriptures were written by men under the _____ of the Holy Spirit.

4. Discuss how the Jews like so many people in our churches today are unable to understand Spiritual truth in the Word.

5. Discuss Paul's spiritual explanation of Moses' commandment in Deuteronomy 22:5:

6. The overarching question today is what part of the law still pertain to the church?

7. Contrast the results of the law being sown into a person's heart versus God's grace planted in the heart.

8. What part of the law pertains to the church?

NOTES

CHAPTER 1

[1]   W.E. Vine's New Testament Greek Grammar Dictionary (Thomas Nelson Publishers 2012) page 442

CHAPTER 3

[2]   W.E. Vine's page 532

CHAPTER 4

[3]   The New King James Study Bible, (Thomas Nelson Publishers 2007) page 1508

[4]   Ibid. page 1509

CHAPTER 10

[5]   W.E. Vine's page 495

[6]   Peter Scazzero, *Emotionally Healthy Spirituality* (Thomas Nelsons, Inc. Nashville, TN 2006) page 16

CHAPTER 14

[7]   D. James Kennedy, *Evangelism Explosion* (Tyndale House Publishers Inc. Wheaton, Illinois 1996)

[8]   W.E. Vine's page 497 Proclamation denotes "a message, a preaching" (the substance of what is "preached" as distinct from the act of "preaching").

[9]   W.E. Vine's page 315 Denotes "doctrine" "teaching"

[10] W.E. Vine's page 347 denotes "communion, fellowship, sharing in common" in 1 Corinthians 19:16.

Printed in the United States
By Bookmasters